CW00428664

Harness the Beast!

Harness the Beast!

**Chris Sellers
& Anton van der Vegt**

MIDDLESEX UNIVERSITY PRESS

Harness the Beast!

The authors

The authors have extensive experience working with large, blue chip multinationals throughout the world. Chris's expertise lies in corporate strategy, change management and continuous improvement, complementing Anton's background as an information systems expert, with numerous patents to his credit. They currently run their own business, Digital Thinking Partners Ltd, providing consultation and training to help companies rapidly improve their business performance by using their existing technology to solve business problems.

The illustrator

David Adamson is a talented cartoonist masquerading as a talented French teacher.

First published in 2002 by Middlesex University Press

Middlesex University Press is an imprint of
MU Ventures Limited,
Bounds Green Road, London N11 2NQ

A CIP catalogue record for this book is available from
The British Library

ISBN   1 898253 51 X

Design by Helen Taylor
Printed by Hobbs the Printers Ltd, Hampshire.

Early praise for *Harness the Beast!*

'Hardly any people in business are aware of the untapped potential for help through the vast range of contemporary IT digital assistance available. The wide availability of high speed broadband makes this omission even more crucial. This book will help to remove the inhibitions and ignorance that hold us back.'

Sir John Harvey-Jones MBE

'Business leaders are looking for answers to their performance issues that do not require yet more investment in systems. The good news is that most are 90% of the way there – all that is missing is a lot of vision, some bridging technologies and knowledgeable support. This book should be both timely and helpful.'

Rick Haythornthwaite, CEO
Invensys plc

'There is an enormous gap between the spend on information technology in our organisations and the potential to be realised in terms of effectiveness. Studies have shown that IT spend has overall not delivered its promised payback. Chris Sellers and Anton van der Vegt show in this book how the gap can be bridged in readable, lively ways animating the concepts and producing, I believe, an animated and committed audience.'

Dr Clive Morton OBE, Chairman
Peterborough Hospitals NHS Trust

'I was disgruntled when I was in the middle of *Harness the Beast!* and realised it applied to me, but by the end I was hungry to get going. Following the simple rules and guidance of *Harness the Beast!* is worth big dollars to my business. I am getting started now.'

Peter Miller, Costs Transformation Leader
BP Grangemouth

'Like the little boy who dared to say the Emperor wasn't wearing any clothes, Sellers and van der Vegt expose the obvious reality which we all seem to deny – we spend a fortune feeding the Beast called technology, but never come close to utilising its full potential. Before you sign another cheque for an even bigger Beast, I suggest that you read this book and learn how to get the most from your current model.'

Martin Boyce, Operations Director
Aerospace Industry

'One of the most valuable lessons I have learnt about managing technology is the importance of focusing not on new hardware and software, but on how people can use them to do things in a different way. Using short case studies to illustrate each point, *Harness the Beast!* offers profound insights in a practical, accessible style with a message that rings true to anyone trying to exploit the full business potential of their information technology.'

John Beattie, Chief Operating Officer
Scottish Centre for Genomic Technology and Informatics

'How relevant all the contents are to my 18 years experience in the manufacturing industry, including most case studies. This book goes beyond the available literature on business tools, organisation efficiency etc. and highlights the enormous potential of untapping and maximising the available information technology to improve organisational efficiency/harmony, profitability and making critical business decisions.

Organisations can be split over assumptions and gut feelings but never over straight facts available from today's under-utilised, costly information technology. This book reveals it all in a simple and practical way. Availability and smart utilisation of available data will be critical for any company's successful and profitable journey into the 21st century.'

Jan Beunder, Product Supply Manager Vietnam
Procter & Gamble

'Your book is fantastic! You should stick it in every airport book store! I think it will be a huge hit. I have read it cover to cover over the last few days and even while reading it, heard all sorts of horror stories from friends' work and at university where people could benefit from the rules for harnessing the

Beast. … Most of the material we were taught last term on this subject was too academic. I like the way *Harness the Beast!* is practical.'

Mark Denton
Australian Graduate School of Management

'*Harness the Beast!* makes you face reality: and what you don't know does hurt you. Forget the force – may the Beast be with you. Simple. Sensible. Practical. A great guide for those who have high-powered jobs in the day but call the kids to work the video at night.'

Tanya Wiley, Lawyer
Acuiti

'What an eye opener!! After years of hearing tales around boardroom tables of the need to invest even more lump sums in IT, often just to get the system to achieve its minimal objectives, I find that simple common sense and positive thinking can harness the IT 'Beast'. That's good news for the bean counters, but even better for those managers who see the potential to move their business forward by utilising the existing IT investment to achieve previously undreamt of results. Well done to the authors for presenting their case in such a readable manner, and the extensive use of case studies encourages each of us to visualise opportunities in our own, supposedly unique, organisations.'

Chairman
Manchester Business School Incubator Ltd

'Reading this book made me realise what a waste of time and money our great new technology has been – but fortunately van der Vegt and Sellers have presented some practical, good sense solutions to help us all get some returns on our Beast!'

Kristin Hay, Regional Human Resources Manager South Asia
MCI WorldCom Asia Pte Ltd

'Thought provoking and potentially controversial, *Harness the Beast!* is a wake-up call to all businesses who think that the solution to their IT problems is to buy more hardware or software. The authors argue convincingly that spending isn't the solution to process faults that ail businesses; rather, the answer is to engage the existing Beast-like IT infrastructure and think your way through existing problems. Many managers will guiltily recognise themselves in these pages as 'the product manager who doesn't even know the name of the systems engineer responsible for his computer system'. After reading *Harness the Beast!* any manager worth their salt will introduce themselves to the systems engineer the very next day, and begin the productive cooperation diagrammed in the book.

Harness the Beast! is a challenge to any manager who thought her area was already producing at the highest level of its capability – and bad news for vendors of software and hardware who promote the 'spend money to solve problems' mentality among their customers.'

Leslie Shannon
Senior IT Project Manager

'In any area of performance improvement, organisations have typically invested heavily in their equipment and in their procedures, but they have overlooked the behavioural aspects – engaging the hearts and minds of their employees. This is just the area of information technology that is addressed in *Harness the Beast!* and not before time.'

Managing Director
Behavioural Science Technology International

Foreword

There are probably no two words more frightening to most executives than Information Technology.

Information Technology held many business executives to ransom in the last decade, as the systems that were supposed to bring transformation to enterprises all too often became major stumbling blocks in making changes.

The real power of this book, and Digital Thinking Partners' approach, is the ability to break the spell of these two words. Written in an engaging voice with real case studies, the seven rules of this book demystify IT and help you understand how to use the *information* held within your *technology* systems to your advantage.

This is not a technology book that tells you what is going on under the hood of your IT systems. The beauty of this book is that it focuses on business problems that have been solved by thinking differently about internal processes and by looking at different ways to extract the information you need from your technology. All too often the data to back up your business decisions or the answer to your strategic problems is lurking within your own IT system; you just need to find a way to get to it.

From wine retail to publishing, I found that most of the problems presented in these entertaining case studies resonated with my own business experience. That is where I found *Harness The Beast!* different from other business books; these stories are from real companies where the seven rules have been tried and tested. Not only does this make the book easy to read and understand, it also helped me to think laterally of different ways to apply the rules across our clients and indeed our own business.

As economic uncertainty spreads and we see spending cuts across many sectors, there is no better time to be thinking differently about getting more out of your existing information and technology. I know from my own experience at *netdecisions*, where we build strategic technology solutions for the world's leading businesses, that this approach works. Our business has grown to 1,000 people in four years by unlocking agility within our clients' IT systems. I wish we had had the benefit of some of the thinking presented in these pages, when we started our business.

Manoj Badale
Co-founder and CEO, netdecisions
Chairman, Agilisys

Harness the Beast!

I can train any dog in five minutes.
It's training the owner that takes longer.

Barbara Woodhouse

Do you ever feel that your job is growing more demanding and less secure? Our business leaders talk about racing towards the digital economy, but this talk doesn't inspire us - it feels more like we're stumbling than racing. Business technology was supposed to be a powerful tool for enhancing our personal performance, providing a competitive advantage and empowering the workforce. Sound familiar?

In the end it feels like more trouble than it's worth. They keep updating software versions, tacking on new systems and sending us off to potted training sessions trying to ensure we're up-to-date, in the loop and on task. Yet we wonder whether the bottom line is really improving. Or worse, we're sinking in information quicksand and drowning in emails.

It helps to think of a computer as a dumb animal. In fact, think of the whole confusion of business technology as the Beast: big and fat and lazy. It's a beast with mammoth, untapped potential. As we conjure this image, we realise that more and more it feels like the Beast's power is dictating the play and constraining our efforts. The Beast thinks it owns the bat and ball and it doesn't always let us play.

And if that's not bad enough, now the economy is wobbling and the bean counters are telling us to cut costs and do more with less. It's no longer enough to trot off to training courses and then rush back to our jobs to continue working in the same way we always have. We have to harness the Beast's awesome power to propel ourselves out of the information quicksand.

Harness the Beast! shows you how to do just that; how to whip the Beast into shape and get it working productively for you by changing the way you approach it.

- **Part One** explains why the enormous power of the Beast has remained largely untapped and what we need to do to harness this power.

- **Part Two** provides seven simple rules for mastering the Beast so that it simplifies your life and gives you the confidence to take the right actions to grab business advantages.

- **Part Three** provides practical advice. Where Part Two demonstrated some of the Beast's capabilities, Part Three helps you harness this potential.

Once you know how, the Beast can be trained relatively easily. It's our training that takes a little longer and not because it's difficult but because it requires us to think differently. Changing our thinking is the essence of harnessing the Beast. The seven simple rules are designed to help you change your thinking.

No matter what job you do, *Harness the Beast!* will demonstrate how you can free up more time to devote to doing it well. No matter what level you operate at, *Harness the Beast!* will have you making smarter decisions. And no matter what business you are in, *Harness the Beast!* will revolutionise that business.

If you've ever been frustrated by the Beast, or if you've ever wondered why the information revolution was beginning to feel like a dud party, then *Harness the Beast!* is for you.

Change your thinking ... harness the Beast.

Contents

Part One Introducing the Beast   **1**

What is the Beast?   2
The evolving Beast   4
The Beast in your business   10
Getting to know the Beast   15

Part Two The Rules   **21**

Rule One The Beast is Accessible   22
Rule Two the Beast is Alive   39
Rule Three The Beast is Mobile   52
Rule Four The Beast is Responsive   67
Rule Five The Beast is Empowering   84
Rule Six The Beast Communicates   106
Rule Seven The Beast is Efficient   123

Part Three Harnessing the Beast   **139**

Seeing the potential   140
Tackling the divide   153
Ready, steady, GO!   172
A message from the authors   178

Appendices   **181**

Digital Health Check   182
Index of case studies   200
Glossary   203
Acknowledgements   205

Part One

Introducing the Beast

What is the Beast?

The computer is a moron.

Peter Drucker

The Beast is an apt metaphor for the ongoing confusion of business technology. By thinking of it as a living, breathing entity, we make dealing with it easier. As a single tangible being it becomes more manageable than the series of intangible connections and unfathomable wires of technical spaghetti looping all around us. Also, the Beast conjures an image of raw power that appropriately reflects the current state of business technology.

And when we say business technology, we mean all the technology existing within your business. Every business has its own unique collection of business technology, its own unique Beast. Most will have PCs containing spreadsheets and other documents, many will include access to local or wide area networks and databases. All businesses have some form of telecommunications – traditional desk bound telephones, the latest mobile phone, or teleconferencing and videoconferencing facilities and even call centres. Some Beasts will include intranet and internet access. However, businesses will also have technology peculiar to them – an oven temperature measuring device, satellite phones or a closed circuit security camera network. These, and other things, are all considered a part of your unique Beast.

We speak of the Beast to make it easier to absorb and think about the topic. Since each business's Beast is unique, it would be awkward to recite a list of technology components under discussion at any single point. Also, when we refer to the Beast in your business, it conjures a more complete image of what is currently available for you to use, rather than limiting your thinking to what you currently use.

Finally, by thinking of business technology as the Beast it becomes easier to conquer and tame. Treating it lightly and with humour makes interacting with it less daunting. Imagining it as a dumb animal encourages us to feel responsible for harnessing its power.

The evolving Beast

A study of economic growth in the US revealed that 70 percent of industries showed no growth despite heavy information technology investment.

McKinsey Report October 2001

Questions are beginning to be asked about the effectiveness of the great technological spend. And if we go down the path of believing that the Beast is a great white elephant, then the information revolution is the world's greatest folly. Billions of pounds have been spent over the last decade alone on business technology infrastructure. Hundreds of thousands of jobs exist to create and sustain this infrastructure and millions of people, just like you, have survived the pain of change to have the Beast in their lives. Can we all have been so wrong?

No, we did not get it wrong, it's just that we haven't got it right... yet. The information revolution is a revolution in progress, not yet complete. The Beast exists not as a great white elephant but as a slumbering behemoth and people are finally realising that technology acquisition alone is not enough – something extra is required. To understand what that extra something is, we must first understand the Beast's evolution.

The insatiable Beast

The focus over the last decade has been on feeding the Beast and very little on harnessing its power. In spite of the vast amounts invested in technology, we have mostly been taught how to use specific applications and have had very little training on how to approach it with new expectations.

Beasts have infiltrated our daily lives yet still they perform mainly routine work. Any moronic computer can run machines, crunch numbers, generate reports and approve transactions. We've got the applications happening but not the revolution.

Companies have invested wildly, believing that without a Beast to call their own they were committing competitive suicide. It became a race where the company with the best Beast wins. But the race has turned into an endurance marathon and we're no longer riding the Beast but instead, carrying it. It sits on our back, bloated yet insatiable, and we pant and groan under the burden of it, wondering where the finishing line is.

But there is no finishing line. Not only is there no finishing line but now we are shackled to this insatiable Beast. It hungrily gobbles our money, our energy, our time and our data, while providing a disproportionately small return. Time spent massaging it to ensure it behaves properly is begrudged and flares our growing irritation and impatience.

Yet since businesses all have access to the same technology components, **competitive advantage will come only from making better use of individual Beasts**.

The Beast's Expenditure

The 1990's was a period of massive expenditure on infrastructure, consulting and implementation, and staff training. In the 1990's in the United States, companies spent $2.2 trillion on information technology[1] and currently in the United Kingdom, the annual information technology spend of publicly listed companies is £43 billion[2] with information technology spending estimated to be about 40 percent of corporate capital spending.[3]

Sources:
1 Business Week Online, 27 Aug 01
2 KPMG News, 27 Sep 01
3 Financial Times, 14 Sep 01

The unharnessed Beast

Let's examine how the Beast evolved in such a way that its potential has gone unharnessed. Every organisation has opportunities to improve. We can represent the scale of this potential as an oval:

The oval of potential

Of course, organisations rarely use all of this potential. How much they use depends on all sorts of artificial, mental constraints: assumptions about what is possible. Such as:

- 'We've always done it this way.'
- 'It seemed to work last time.'
- Out dated company policies.
- Departmental boundaries.

We can depict an area within our *oval of potential*, bounded by all these constraints, to represent the improvement potential being used by the people in the organisation.

Opportunity bounded by mental constraints

Now, all that happens when we invest in technology is that we greatly expand the potential for improvement i.e. we enlarge the *oval of potential*. It doesn't necessarily follow that people perceive the constraints to have moved, so the inner shape does not alter. Assumptions about what is possible remain unchanged.

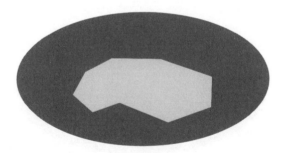

New technology increases oval of potential

What we can end up with is no change in the way we work. The only sure change is that we are surrounded by a massive potential to improve – opportunities waiting to be discovered.

Of course, the organisation will change some of its work practices. However, typically only a few of the constraints get moved.

Only a few constraints get moved

This means that a massive opportunity exists for the organisation to use this additional potential it has invested in. The key to really grasping this potential for improvement is no longer in implementation of technology – this has already far outstripped the use we make of it – it lies in removing the constraints that stop people from seeing and making the most of the potential. The key is to change assumptions about what is possible.

Push back the constraints

This opportunity exists everywhere, in every business, at every level. As you will find out in Part Two, these are opportunities that require no further capital investment or changing of business goals. They are opportunities waiting to be discovered, if only you can change your assumptions about what is possible.

Potential harnessed

The new big lever

Spend is no longer the big lever. Since we are not already using the Beast's full potential, we won't reach our digital nirvana simply by throwing more money at it. Tapping into this unharnessed power requires no new capital investment. The new big lever involves using existing technology better: working smarter by making the Beast work harder.

Early on, the Beast required large capital injections to develop its infrastructure and the resultant spend acted like a big lever, producing big results. However, now the Beast has grown to a size where the return curve is flattening. The new big lever is thinking.

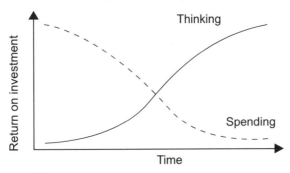

The next big step change in the Beast's payback will come from improved thinking. We call this improved thinking *digital thinking* and it will greatly contribute to increasing the Beast's performance. Then, when we understand the Beast and have it fully harnessed, future spends will be better directed and made with greater confidence. The Beast's evolution will then continue smoothly.

The Beast in your business

> *An informal poll of UK finance directors found that a majority was preoccupied with controlling and managing the flow of information and ensuring information technology systems were properly integrated throughout the business.*
>
> Accountancy, July 2001

So what are our constraining assumptions, and why haven't they changed? We touched on it earlier when we mentioned cries of *'We've always done it this way'*, assumptions about what is possible, outdated policies and departmental boundaries. However, more fundamentally, the assumptions we have failed to change stem from our attitudes towards our Beast, our relationship with the Beast's keepers, and our limited approach about the way we do our jobs.

These three things combine to constrain our assumptions about what is possible. If we don't understand what is possible, it cannot be pursued. If we don't understand what is possible, we cannot ask for it to happen. And if we cannot ask for it happen, it will not happen.

You and the Beast

Embracing the Beast is not something most of us do naturally or easily, so making the most of the Beast is doubly difficult when we haven't fully mastered the conceptual shift required by the information revolution.

Imagine the conceptual shift required in making the revolutionary step from radio to television without adjusting our approach to this new technology. For example, we've tuned in for our favourite football team playing a greatly anticipated match but the picture is turned off and only the sound is working. Perhaps the salesman mentioned that the new box delivered pictures too. Maybe we even witnessed a demonstration. But the picture button accidentally got turned down and we're too involved in the game to interrupt it and start messing about with all those mysterious knobs. Besides, we're still getting as much as we're used to – we're still hearing the game.

If you think this analogy is too simplistic, then cast a thought to your video remote control. How many buttons does it have? Now count how many you know how to use and how many you regularly use. There's probably a large difference between the first number and the last. This is a better analogy because it demonstrates the under utilisation of a common appliance. But it's not about learning to push more buttons. It's about knowing what the Beast can do. We need to know what all those buttons on the video remote control can do before we can decide which ones are useful.

It took the television 26 years to get into 25% of all US homes, whereas it took the internet only seven years.

The pace of technological change is quickening too. If we still haven't mastered our video remote controls, it's little wonder that our Beast is wandering around unharnessed.

The coming of the Beast has changed the game, yet most of us are still playing with the old rules. We're merely using the Beast as an improved applications tool – we have the picture turned off but *Hey, the sound's great!* Even though everyone may have undertaken the same basic training on how to interact with the Beast, how to get it to perform its tricks, we all exit the training with differing levels of competence in handling the Beast. This basic training typically doesn't teach us how to think differently.

Our resultant attitude is that it is not our place to harness the Beast. Like most people, we merely go along for the ride. We are not trained in how to maximise the Beast's power, nor are we trained to become digital thinkers. And that means using only a fraction of the Beast's potential.

This is important because it goes towards explaining part of the reason why we are currently making so little use of the Beast's power. We don't believe it is our responsibility. We believe it is the responsibility of the Beast's keepers. But who are they?

The Beastkeepers

We assume that it is the job of others to harness our Beast. These *others* we find buzzing away in the Information Technology Department, or they are the information gatekeepers, knowledge managers, or the accountants who produce reports. Collectively, let's refer to them as the Beastkeepers.

We assume the Beastkeepers are responsible for bringing the Beast to life, nurturing it and making it accountable. We assume the Beastkeepers should be ensuring we get the most from our Beast.

It's not our job to understand the ins and outs of the Beast. Nor is it our job to understand the capabilities of this latest piece of technological kit. It is also not our job to ensure this fresh imposition is put to best use. It is our job to secure sales, or communicate with our customer base, or to manage the production line, keep the books balanced, order the supplies and so on. It's the job of the Beastkeepers to manage the Beast. Or so we assume.

That assumption constrains the way we do our job. The result of our collective assumption is that as the information revolution rolled over us, it created a functional divide. The Beastkeepers do their thing and we do ours. Business technology is something the Beastkeepers periodically impose on the business under the guise of progress or improvement. They use phrases like *We must meet new compliance standards* and *The current system will be unsupported in two years time*, to explain these impositions. But to us these impositions are usually painful and disruptive hurdles to overcome before we can get back to the important business of doing our job. And we get on with that job without changing our assumptions about what is possible or about who should realise the potential.

The Business/Beastkeeper Divide

Our assumption, that the Beastkeepers are responsible for harnessing the Beast's potential, creates a functional divide between business and information technology (IT). Or perhaps, to be more accurate, we should call it a dysfunctional divide.

This divide, with the Beastkeepers doing their thing and us doing ours, means that the Beastkeepers' objectives and our business objectives often operate in parallel. Being able to harness the Beast's power means being able to bridge the divide between these parallel, and sometimes opposing, sets of objectives.

The ubiquitous Beast is complicated and high maintenance, and demands a great deal of specialist care and attention. There are as many types of Beastkeepers providing this specialist care as there are components of the Beast. They are experts in their particular field.

Just as we attend to our jobs, looking after customers, production lines or accounting records, they are attending to their jobs by keeping the network functioning, writing software, installing PCs or updating anti-virus protection and so on.

Of course, the most senior Beastkeepers will have one eye on the business's objectives, just as our senior business leaders do. However, these objectives must filter down to the day-to-day, implementation and maintenance level Beastkeepers, just as they filter down our (parallel) chain of command. Often there are very few open channels of communication on the way down, between business and IT. Where open channels do exist… well, the Beastkeepers speak a different language, one that we cannot always comprehend.

It is a self-perpetuating situation. Since we don't speak the language of the Beast we struggle to understand the Beast's potential and the Beastkeepers struggle to tell us. As the Beastkeepers speak in a different language, we struggle to articulate our business needs and communication channels shrivel. So the functional divide continues, us busy with our jobs and the Beastkeepers busy with theirs, and the Beast going largely unharnessed.

So whose responsibility is it to get the Beast to earn its keep? The best way to respond to that question is to reframe it. Whilst it isn't our job to ensure the Beast's productivity, it is our responsibility to ensure we do the best job we can, *given the available resources*. The Beast is a powerful, under-utilised resource.

As you will see in Part Two, the benefits of harnessing the Beast are significant and varied, from cost reduction and increased profitability, to improved efficiencies and greater personal impact. In Part Three, we discuss ways of tackling this business/Beastkeeper divide.

By changing our assumptions about what is possible, and learning to bridge the business/Beastkeeper divide, you can better understand your Beast's potential and discover the hidden opportunities within your business.

Getting to know the Beast

> *The typical company has made 80% of the investment in the technology that can give it a healthy flow of information yet is typically getting only 20% of the benefits that are now possible.*
>
> Bill Gates

The need for rules

We mentioned earlier that the assumptions we have failed to change stem from our attitudes towards our Beast, our relationship with the Beast's keepers, and our constraints about the way we do our job. We assume it is the responsibility of the Beastkeepers to harness the Beast yet we carry on poor communications with them to the point of sustaining a functional divide.

However, only we, who know the objectives and problems of our business, can make the necessary changes. It is by yoking our business insight to the Beastkeepers' knowledge that we can harness the Beast's power.

First we need to change our constraints to provide a new set of assumptions from which to work. We need to become digital thinkers. Yet making conceptual changes to our thinking can be difficult, particularly when our personal circumstances, our industries, our businesses and our positions are as different as our Beasts.

Therefore, the provision of a new set of assumptions needs to be generic yet comprehensive, insightful yet simple. What follows are seven rules for harnessing your Beast. They provide a framework for changing your assumptions.

Applying the rules

The case studies* are based on the authors' experiences of working to help a wide range of businesses across the world to solve business problems or improve efficiencies. Extensive access to a wide cross-section of business activity enabled them to identify patterns in the near universal failure of businesses to optimise the potential of the Beast.

Subsequently, the rules were developed as an aid to smashing old assumptions about what is possible. These rules function as mindset-breakers, putting in place a new set of assumptions about your Beast's potential. Applying each rule is about assuming one thing in order to open up many possibilities. It's a way of leveraging the Beast's power.

The rules are designed to simplify a complex subject and the case studies have been selected to cover a range of situations. Together, the rules and the case studies aim to start you on the path to becoming a digital thinker. The more you apply the rules, the more the changes in your assumptions will become ingrained and, unlike rote learning, it's not about remembering which button to press, it's about an attitude, an approach that won't be forgotten and can't be unlearned.

The rules are explained in Part Two. Each chapter explains a single

---

* For confidentiality reasons, identifying details have been altered and, where necessary, extraneous details have been excluded.

rule and provides case studies demonstrating different ways of successfully interpreting the rule. Part Three shows you how to successfully apply them by tackling the business/Beastkeeper divide. Together, parts two and three teach you how to pull the new big lever.

The Rules

Rule One   **The Beast is Accessible**
Information is available to everyone who needs it, in an accessible format.

Rule Two   **The Beast is Alive**
Information is available live.
We don't have to wait for a post-mortem to make decisions.

Rule Three   **The Beast is Mobile**
The world is our workplace.
Geography and location are irrelevant.

Rule Four   **The Beast is Responsive**
Feedback and organisational response are instant.

Rule Five   **The Beast is Empowering**
Better business decisions are made with greater confidence.

Rule Six   **The Beast Communicates**
Effective communication is easy.

Rule Seven   **The Beast is Efficient**
Data is captured and stored once.

The Eco Plastics Story

The story of Eco Plastics is used throughout the book to provide a different way of thinking about the rules and other concepts under discussion. The story is a stand-alone feature which may be skipped without detriment to comprehension.

The Eco Plastics Story

Together Peter, Gus and Kate run a medium-size plastics recycling company. Peter and Gus run the day-to-day production and sales side of the business whilst Kate looks after the numbers. The market had been buoyant for several years and everything had been going smoothly, but suddenly the market had changed dramatically with a rise in imports as well as reduced local margins. It was time for an urgent management meeting...

Kate was worried about the company's declining financial situation. The bottom was falling out of the recycled plastic business. Increased scrap purchase prices, increased government intervention and charges, and increased foreign competition were tolling the death knell.

'How do I make this penetrate? We are haemorrhaging!' Kate slid the monthly report across the boardroom table towards Peter but it stopped short.

'Then we'll pump up the volume.' He made no attempt to retrieve the report, happy to keep it at arm's length from the argument.

'Look at the numbers.' Kate now seemed to be talking to her abandoned report. 'All this low margin work is killing us. We need to cut costs.'

Gus cleared his throat, an unconscious habit indicating he was about to join the discussion. 'Sorry Peter, I agree with Kate on this one. We need to control our costs better.'

Peter let out one of his patronising sighs. 'I've been in the recycling game longer than you two put together. We don't owe anything against the business so all we have to do is increase productivity. Any fool can tell you that.'

'Our electricity usage has suddenly shot up by 15 percent. We need to understand why. We've got to control our costs.' Gus looked to Kate for backup.

'I agree controlling costs is the way to go but what I had in mind

CASE STUDY

CASE STUDY

was reducing labour costs and wastage. We could go to a four-day week.' Kate pulled a document from her folder. 'I've prepared some numbers and …'

'Take that strategy to its logical conclusion and we'll disappear up our own backsides!' Peter was in no mood for more of Kate's numbers.

'If it's waste you're concerned about Kate, I have an idea for a new extruded waste by-product,' Gus chipped in, 'all we have to do is find a market for it.'

'That sounds good.' Peter looked impressed but Kate was horrified.

'We don't have time for faffing about with new product development. You two aren't listening. We are haemorrhaging!'

Part Two

The Rules

The Beast is Accessible

Information is available to everyone who needs it, in an accessible format.

Business success is 1% inspiration and 99% information.

Anon

When our groceries are scanned at the checkout we are feeding the supermarket's Beast. When we pre-book cinema tickets we are providing the cinema and film distributors with marketing information. Every internet site we access, every form we complete is recorded deep in some Beast's bowels. The Beast is crammed with all sorts of information but how often do we think about accessing it when going about our everyday lives?

We seem to have two different mindsets when it comes to providing and accessing information. Most people have come to terms with the fact (albeit grudgingly) that they are a major source of companies' data, but few think to access information that would prove valuable, even when they know it exists. Probably, because they don't think of it as theirs, they don't believe they can access it.

Of course some information is sensitive or personal and quite rightly is protected and should not be accessible to everyone. However, there is a great deal of information that does not fall into this category and would indeed be useful if only we thought to ask for it.

It is important to acknowledge there are two major aspects of accessibility that must be addressed if we are to make the most of the Beast. The first is whether or not we believe the information can be reached. If it resides on another system, in another department, in another country, we often ignore it as a potential source. This is a throw-back to the times before the Beast, when systems were totally discrete and connectivity or transmission of data was fraught with difficulties. With the advent of database standards and the internet, there is little that cannot be searched for, selected and sent anywhere in the world.

The second is whether or not the data is in a format that makes sense to us. This is a huge block for many people. They know the information exists but don't expect to be able to understand it, so dismiss it. However, the Beast can relatively easily provide this information in many different formats, from lists of numbers to complex three-dimensional graphs.

So, just consider for a moment how many times we make decisions, often really important decisions, without information that would help us get it right. If we truly believe that the Beast is accessible, that we could get any information we needed in a format we understood, it follows that we would make more informed decisions, be able to show people why what we say is right, foresee pitfalls and grasp opportunities. It's better to limit guesswork and intuition to those situations that are truly unknown and minimise the risk in our decision making by tapping into what the Beast already knows!

More wine please

For the majority of us wine represents social time, relaxation, and celebrations. However, for John it is serious business. John works for a large chain of wine shops and his job is to help the individual outlets increase sales. Specifically, he does this by creating shelf plans. A shelf plan is a detailed specification of shelf stocking for wines that the company is promoting.

John is responsible for a particular area of the country and must create shelf plans for each of the 145 shops in his large and diverse area, which covers both cities and small country towns.

We asked John to explain what he does.

'Each year I produce a single shelf plan for each shop. Unfortunately, each shop has a unique layout so, whilst there are similarities, no two are identical. When I've completed the shelf plan, I send it to the shop and they rearrange the shelf stock to match it.'

'Do all shelf plans go out together?'

'No, not at all. I work my way through the list of shops and, as soon as the shelf plan is ready, I send it out, so each of the shops receive theirs at different times during the year.'

'Where did this idea come from, John?'

'Four years ago we got a new marketing director who was new to the wine business and had previously worked in hardware. He'd seen this type of exercise work in his old company so we did a couple of trials and they worked well. The shop managers enjoyed trying something new and sales lifted during the trials, so he set up the team I'm now working in.' John waved his hand at the cluster of nearby desks. 'Five of us produce shelf plans for the whole country.'

'Sounds good. Your team must impact significantly on the company's performance.'

'Well…maybe.' John replied sheepishly.

'You sound unsure.'

'Trials are one thing but now that shelf plans go out to every shop we do have a few problems'

'Like what?'

'Some shops don't like doing them. In fact some of the shop managers can get really rude about them. I wouldn't mind but they take it out on us. I tell them we're just doing our job and it's not us they should complain to, but it doesn't seem to help. Each of us has our list of shops that we dread contacting each year because we know they'll give us a hard time.'

'So what do they complain about?'

'They say our shelf plans are a waste of time. They don't believe they increase sales at all and some shops even reckon they reduce sales. What can I say? Several don't bother implementing the shelf plans. And who would know? My area is so large with so many shops that I only get to my local ones. My most distant shop is 200 miles away. If they don't want to implement my shelf plan there's nothing I can do about it. It shouldn't get us down, they're all entitled to their opinion, but when you've spent hours carefully preparing it, only to be told they put it straight in the bin ... I mean, life's too short isn't it?' John looked despondent.

'So the disagreement is always about whether or not the shelf plan has an impact on sales?'

'That's right.'

'Well, don't you have the sales information to prove the impact?'

'No, we don't have any of that information.'

Do you think the information exists somewhere in your organisation?

We challenged John's assumption by asking whether he thought the information existed somewhere in his organisation. He considered this for some time, musing that since the company installed an electronic till system a couple of years ago, it records every sale and allows the warehouse to automatically redeliver stock. John had never seen the information though and was adamant that the marketing department wasn't collecting it. We prompted him to think about how he might find out exactly what information the warehouse system held and whether it had the information he needed.

As it turned out, John played basketball with someone from the warehouse and, although he didn't know exactly what data existed, he knew someone who did, called Jolanda.

John explained to Jolanda that he needed to know whether shelf plans impacted on sales. She happily talked him through what data was collected, the reports that were generated and how they were used in the warehouse.

'The weekly sales by shop sounds like the report I need,' said John. 'I don't need all the detail you require in the warehouse but if I can separate stock wines and promotional wines that could be interesting.'

'No problem. That's all in the standard weekly report. I'll send over a copy of last week's so you can see what it looks like and then, if it helps, I'll put you on the email distribution list so you get it each Friday.'

John was excited. Being able to prove the impact of shelf plans would mean that, rather than arguing with shop managers about what the impact might be, he could discuss the actual impact. He decided to use the first report Jolanda sent to assess the shelf plans from the last two months. The results were surprising.

Most shops showed a positive impact, some had no change in sales, and a couple actually showed a negative impact. John talked with every shop manager in an attempt to understand these mixed results. His initial discussions told him that there seemed to be a correlation between the type of client and the effectiveness of the shelf plan.

Over the next few weeks John established that the shops in his area fell into two broad groups:

- Shops where shelf plans had a positive impact, and

- Shops where shelf plans had a negative impact.

For the shops where sales were unchanged, it was due to the shop managers not implementing the shelf plans, believing them to be bad for business.

From discussions with the managers and by comparing the locations of the shops in the two broad groups, John realised that the current shelf plans, which introduced new products, worked well in the central city areas where the customers had lots of choice about where to buy. The city managers liked the shelf plans and saw them as integral to attracting people into the shop.

The shops in country towns or small city suburbs, where the customer base was more regular, found that customers would come in anyway and the changes made in implementing the shelf plans actually confused customers rather than stimulated them. For these shops the buying patterns were usually much better defined and their customers didn't stray too far from the products they knew and liked. They agreed it was important to make changes during the year, in fact they usually did this themselves anyway but their customers seemed to want less radical change.

John's team decided to produce two different types of shelf plans. The first was similar to the existing ones, where really different products are introduced. This was mainly for the big stores where being up with the latest trends and attracting people is critical. The second took a different approach to satisfy stores that needed to build upon existing sales patterns. In this case, shelf plans introduced new products by placing them next to complementary or similar ones, and made other changes more subtly.

More importantly, the impact of shelf plans would now be monitored routinely so everybody would know what was working and what was not.

Over the next six months, John and his team worked with the shop managers to refine the shelf plan process so that the large city stores received two of the 'radical' shelf plans each year rather than one. The others continued to receive one per year but one that was more subtle, with change based on their existing sales pattern.

The relationship between John's department and the shops it services has improved. In John's words: *We're actually having constructive conversations with those we previously saw as our most difficult managers!*

This change not only significantly improved the working relationships within the company but also had a positive impact on sales. From John's analysis, he can now prove that whilst overall, last year's shelf plans had a positive impact, the new approach increased sales by a further 3 percent. And that's a lot of wine!

INSIGHTS

- John knew what information he needed. He even knew the company probably had it. But because a different department collected it, he assumed it was inaccessible to him.

- John and his team spent all year making shelf plans yet were unsure of their impact. It was a good idea, poorly communicated. With no measures of success it meant the idea significantly under-performed its potential for several years.

Making it happen

Daniel and Charles run a boutique management consultancy providing cost reduction expertise to clients.

The business of management consulting is to help other people's businesses succeed. However, Daniel and Charles had a major challenge to get their own business right. The office they ran was part of a global company and, as with all the offices, they were under mounting pressure to increase profits through growth.

Over the last two years, their revenue had remained stagnant whilst the salary bill had increased in the never-ending challenge to attract and retain the best talent. Therefore profits had dropped by 20 percent. This is unsustainable in the enormously competitive arena of management consulting where perform or out is the understood norm. There is no shortage of talented individuals in their global organisation and, if things didn't improve, it had been made clear that there were others who could make it happen.

'From the outside you'd think this would be a simple business to run. Low overheads, high differentials between billing rates and salaries, talented employees and a large number of potential clients.' When Daniel stopped talking Charles took over.

'The thing is that all we have is our people. The quality of the job they do each day when they're with a client is all-important. That's why we've invested so much time and effort over the last twelve months in consultant development, helping them work on their client interaction skills as well as the specialist skills required in cost reduction initiatives.'

We asked whether this had improved the situation.

'Yes and no,' said Daniel, 'our client relationships are definitely better. In the last six months we've had no projects where the client has brought it to an abrupt end because they weren't satisfied with the consultants' performances. However, our employees have become more valuable and so we have had to increase salaries to keep them. In fact we've lost two of our most senior consultants to rivals and I know others have been approached.' Daniel shrugged his shoulders in despair.

'We have no issue with paying our consultants well but we need to increase our profits to make this possible,' Charles added quickly.

The downward spiral was clear: invest heavily in your people, fail to improve profits, lose your best people, then either invest more heavily in your people or risk damaging client relationships. Obviously just investing in their people hadn't directly increased profits. Indeed, it had a positive impact on client relationships but they now needed a profit increase to complement and stabilise the situation.

'Okay, so increasing profit is your big question. What are the main levers on profit for your business?'

'The maths is simple,' explained Charles as he passed over the monthly report. 'As we said, all we have are our people, so revenue is determined by this equation.' He scribbled on his notepad:

$$Billing\ rate \times utilisation \times number\ of\ consultants = Revenue$$

'As our costs are almost all fixed, if the revenue goes up, the profit goes up and so these are the variables we graph on our monthly report.'

The utilisation level was bouncing around 50-60 percent against a target of 75 percent. The number of consultants was fairly steady at thirty, fluctuating by plus or minus two during the year. We had expected the billing rate to be rock steady but that too fluctuated.

'Why does the billing rate fluctuate so much? We thought you would have a fixed rate?'

'Depends on the client, the potential payback of the project and the economic climate. We have to find a rate that's reasonable. It's part of the up-front negotiation.'

Whilst this monthly report gave a good picture of how well the business was doing in terms of these critical levers, it didn't help us understand what needed to be done to improve them. For instance, the decision to invest in consultant development was made for all the right reasons but this report didn't guide that decision. The development decision was based on the assumption that improving consultants' interaction with the clients would improve profits. This assumption proved inaccurate.

What we needed to do was dig a bit deeper and see if there were any clues as to how best to increase profits.

We started to explore this with Daniel and Charles but there seemed to be a hesitation on their part.

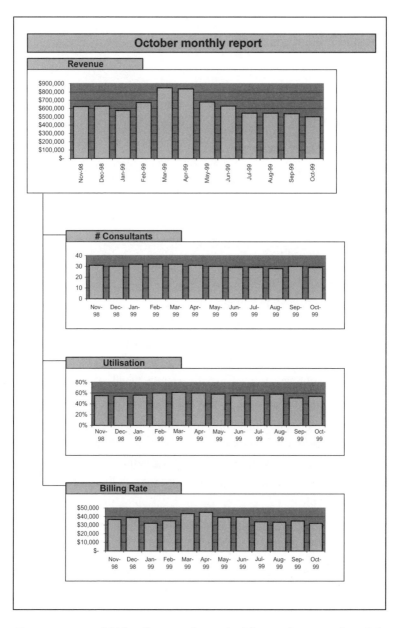

'I'm sure we could identify some theoretical factors but even if we did, there's a fair chance they'd be immeasurable. Our business is so human centred that it's more like an art than a science. And if we did find something we could measure we don't have time to start measuring and waiting for results. We need to show a believable plan to Head Office by next week.'

Suspend belief and assume the information exists.

We talked this concern through for a while before asking them to suspend their belief and assume for the moment that if they could identify factors, then the supporting data would exist. The conversation centred on trying to understand what things really determined the three factors: billing rate, utilisation and number of consultants, and how to find out how big an impact these things might have. Eventually we came to the following conclusions:

- **Billing rate** was likely to be determined by industry sector and project payback potential.

- **Utilisation** for an individual was likely to be determined by the number of times they finished projects during a year, as it was the gaps between projects that were the greatest source of loss. The inverse of this is to measure the average length of projects.

- **Number of consultants** was very much in the hands of Charles and Daniel as they had full responsibility for hiring and firing. The key driver for them was to hire when they expected the utilisation to increase to ensure sufficient demand for their services. Although indirectly, number of employees is therefore driven by utilisation.

'Okay, so if these are likely factors, we need to find out if they really do have a significant impact. So what information do we have?'

'Well, this report is our main source of information. That comes from accounts, but doesn't help with this.' Daniel again brandished the monthly report. 'Let's just think, where can we get it?'

They decided to discuss their information needs with Jen, the Accounts Manager, and discovered that the system actually had significantly more information than was shown on the monthly report.

Jen explained that, because every consultant must complete timesheets against given jobs, she sets up a code for each project which gets opened when the project starts and closed when it finishes. This meant she could easily provide information about the duration of projects by client.

Daniel and Charles seemed pleasantly surprised.

Jen continued. 'From the same data we can also extract the number of consultants on a project, if that helps. You should talk to Lindsay about the other things you need. She collates loads of information on prospective client companies when she's doing the marketing.'

Lindsay proved a great source of information. Her marketing contacts database stored not only contact details but also the industry classification, company turnover, number of employees, whether it was national or international and so on.

'I hadn't really thought about all the different information we collect.' Daniel reflected. 'It'll be interesting to see if there's any correlation between some of this data and our key levers.'

Daniel got a system dump of the appropriate data for the last thirty-six months from both Jen and Lindsay and set about compiling it into a spreadsheet. What he found was certainly enlightening.

Daniel talked us through the graphs. 'I knew there were differences between clients and industries but I never realised they were so significant. It's fascinating to see that potential payback is not a big factor on the billing rate. The rate appears to be determined by the accepted norm for that industry.'

"Our strategy becomes a lot clearer now. We should focus on clients who are comfortable with long consulting projects, industry sectors where the accepted billing rate is high and large clients who require several consultants to deliver a project.'

'It certainly changes a few priorities for us,' Charles agreed. We need to re-look at who we are planning to sell more business to and be much more proactive with those clients who are likely to give better returns. What's great is that we can explain both to Head Office and our own consultants just why we are taking this approach.'

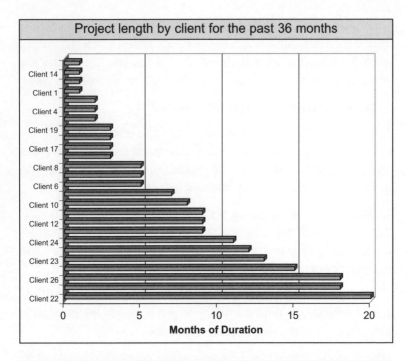

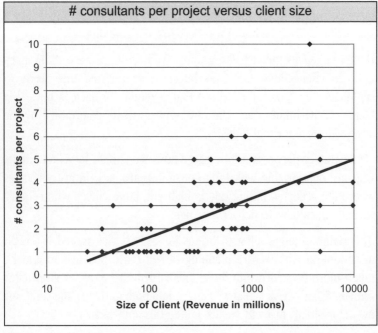

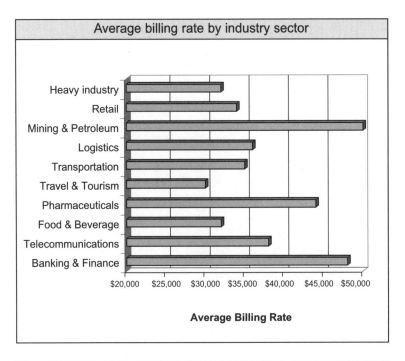

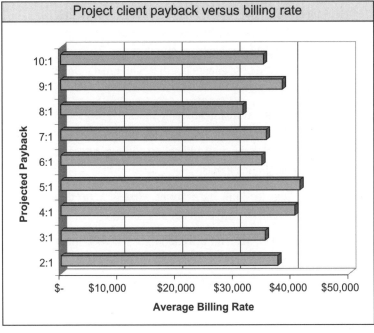

It still took a while to turn the business around but eighteen months later the monthly revenue had increased by 83 percent thanks to utilisation reaching 73 percent. The average billing rate climbed from $37,000 to $45,000 per month and the number of consultants increased to thirty-four. As the fixed costs had not increased significantly, the profit increase was even better, spring-boarding them into the top quartile of their company offices.

'We haven't yet achieved our utilisation target but that should happen in the next couple of months. The best news is that our profits have trebled. All because we decided to look hard at which clients were best for us. What has been most interesting is that we didn't need to grow very much either. The key wasn't growth after all but return on our effort. Now the people at Head Office are asking us how we made it happen and that's a nice change!'

INSIGHTS

- Daniel and Charles were used to analysing other businesses but when it came to their own they accepted what information they were given and based critical decisions on assumptions. They may be big-brain consultants but that didn't make them digital thinkers.

- They didn't fundamentally believe the evidence existed so could not see why they should consider the factors impacting utilisation, billing rate and number of consultants.

- They had to think hard about what they needed before realising the evidence may exist.

- In fact all the data they needed did exist, just not in one place.

Rule One Summary

- The biggest challenges to information flow are organisational and mental, not technical.

- The people who 'own' information cannot be expected to know you need it.

- Assume everything is accessible and force yourself to work out what you really need.

- Ask for information to be provided in a format that you can work with.

- Prepare to be surprised at what exists!

Thinking about your Beast

- How often during this week have you made decisions based on assumptions rather than facts?

- How many of these decisions could have been backed by information but because it is held somewhere else you ignored it?

- How much more confidence in your decision would you and others have had if it had been accompanied with supporting evidence?

- How many of your actions stalled because, without evidence, you couldn't convince others of the need?

- Try to live by the rule, use questions such as these to help challenge yourself:

  - Have I assumed information exists?

  - Have I thought: Who might have what I need?

  - Am I clear on what I need, before I ask?

The Eco Plastics Story

As Production Manager, Gus didn't normally look too closely at Kate's monthly reports. All those columns of numbers he found soporific. He trusted Kate to do her job and keep the accounting straight, and trusted Peter to handle the business side of affairs. In the past, he had trusted himself not to come between the two of them during directors' meetings. However, lately their stress levels had spiked as much as their electricity bills and Gus felt it was time he took on more responsibility.

That's why, at 11.00 on a Sunday evening, he was trying not to fall asleep over Kate's latest report. Determined to do his bit to save Eco Plastics, he decided to pursue his waste by-product idea and was working backwards from Kate's report, trying to calculate product profitability. He wanted to work out whether the idea was viable but was struggling to extract the figures he needed. The report seemed confined to average price per unit and average cost per unit figures. He couldn't work out from this what he needed to know. He decided to sleep on it.

In the morning he sought out Peter and asked him how he calculates a product's profitability. Peter explained that it's not as easy as it might at first seem because the cost of their raw material (scrap) fluctuates daily. This price fluctuation cannot always be passed on though because the sale price is capped by the cost of virgin product. If Eco Plastics' customers can source non-recycled materials for X amount, then recycled plastics must be priced less than X to remain viable.

Peter explained that it's even more complicated for any waste by-product because it will come from a range of core products. Although there are only five core productions, each has a number of variations, so the total number of products is almost thirty.

'Why don't you ask Kate to do a preliminary crunching of the numbers for you?'

The Beast is Alive

**Information is available live.
We don't have to wait for a post-mortem
to make decisions.**

---

*Improvements from better and more
timely information are 'never less than
20 percent, often a 50 percent change,
and sometimes ... as high as six fold.'*

Thomas Gilbert

When we say the Beast is alive we mean that the data it holds is constantly available, if only we learn to ask for it in real time. We don't have to wait for an information post-mortem to make a decision or alter the game plan. Too often information is used to find out what went wrong, or worse, simply to learn that *something* went wrong.

If the information supplied to you makes you feel like you're looking in a rear view mirror it's probably because you are. Whilst it may be interesting to see where you've been it is not always relevant to the road ahead. Have you ever wasted time trying to explain a graph fluctuation that occurred weeks ago? And have you ever felt foolish for not being able to explain the fluctuation?

The Beast knew all about that graph fluctuation at the time it happened, but you didn't ask. And you didn't ask because you probably assumed it wasn't possible for the Beast to tell you so quickly. This is not your fault, nor the Beast's, nor the Beastkeepers'. It's just applying old thinking instead of digital thinking.

But there's another reason too, one that must be aired. There can be a strange comfort in not knowing about that graph fluctuation immediately. If we knew immediately that something had just gone wrong, we just might be expected to fix it immediately… and we've never been able to understand that particular problem. Better not to fail so obviously and immediately when we can drip feed our failure over months and years and seemingly dilute its ramifications.

Deep down everyone knows that when we get the report a week late there is little chance of us fixing the problem if we haven't already. The report arrives too late to do anything other than allow management to point out the problem and ask a few probing questions so they are seen to be in control.

Whatever the reason though, it is unacceptable now that we know that the Beast is alive. It is also unnecessary because, since the Beast is alive, we can set it to work.

Look around your business, whatever it might be and you will find examples where this rule is overlooked, where information is out of date by the time it reaches the people who could do something about it. People are so busy trying to explain last month's performance they are not optimising this week's tasks. Unnecessary delays occur because the old way of thinking about our jobs still dominates, even though we often believe that we have 'gone digital'.

'Going digital' is not digital thinking

Take Jane for instance. Jane is an experienced data processing clerk. There is nothing Jane does not know about her job. She's been doing it for two years, and regularly breaks records for the number of accounts she can process in a day. When she started her job the new system had only just been put in and nobody knew how to work it. Jane had used computers in her last job and was really comfortable working out how to get the new system to process accounts that were previously handled manually. Within a day she was the team expert. *Jane, how do I do this? Jane, pleeease help me. What does this error message mean?*

Two years on and everyone has the hang of the new system. The department is proudly heralded as a shining example of using technology to improve performance. Jane's team regularly handles twice as many accounts each week as the department previously handled manually. No more improvements to be had here. It looks fully digital. What value could rules for harnessing the Beast contribute?

We asked Jane to take us through her data processing job.

'We have two steps to complete for each of these accounts so they can be transferred from the old network to the new one.' Jane explained patiently, clearly having honed her story many times and pitching it just right for total novices. 'I receive the account details as an attachment to an email.' To show us, her fingers flew across the keyboard, the screen changing several times, challenging us to keep up. 'I collect up a batch of roughly fifty accounts and set them off on the first step which cleans up the batch and cross checks against our database.'

'Why fifty?' we asked, stalling for time so we could catch up on all her rapid fire screen changes.

'Just experience. I've found that fifty is about the optimal. The system manual says we should use batches of 300.' Jane rolled her eyes. 'But if you do that, and there's a problem, you've wasted at least two hours.'

'What do you mean, if there's a problem?'

'It's never anything complicated. It's just that occasionally we get a bad batch. Lots of non-standard stuff like tabs instead of spaces, that sort of thing. Generally they're consistent faults. If one account fails, all of the ones in that batch fail.'

'Is it difficult to fix?'

'It's fiddly and very frustrating. Until the system has finished going through all the accounts in that batch you don't know there's a problem. That's why we do batches of fifty because it saves time. If we did 300 like the manual says, it would take two hours for the system to run it and then reject it. We were under a lot of pressure early on from the systems guy to run the 300 batch size because he reckons the processing is more efficient – 20 percent faster, he says. But if it fails, that's two hours wasted.'

'Can't you do a quality check before running them? Spot the failures before they happen?'

'Tried that. It took us so long to check each batch that it was quicker to skip the checks and deal with the odd one that goes wrong.'

'How often do they fail?'

'About once a day. I average about twenty batches a day so that's only one in twenty.'

'Exactly what happens when a batch fails?'

'The computer generates a log after each batch.' Jane reached for one to show us. 'As you can see, for each account it processes, the computer appends a line to the log saying whether it worked or failed.'

'And you get this log at the end of the batch?'

'That's right.'

'And if it's a bad batch each account will come up as failed?'

'Correct.'

When does the computer know an account has failed?

We asked Jane when the computer knew that an account had failed. She had to think about that, finally confessing that she didn't know 'the ins and outs of how the system operates'. She chewed over it a moment longer. 'I could ask the systems guy if you think it makes a difference.'

'Well, it would if the computer told you as soon as an account failed, rather than writing it all to the log and handing it over at the end, because then you could interrupt a batch when you saw all the accounts failing.'

Jane's face lit up. 'That's a good idea. I'll ask the systems guy if we can see the log as it is written.'

Jane asked the systems guy whether she could view the log in real time and found that it could be done with only a couple of keystrokes. The next day Jane broke her own record after catching a bad batch only five minutes into the run, rather than waiting thirty minutes until the end. Two days later she increased her batch size to 300 and grabbed another 20 percent improvement.

Over the next week Jane taught her five team-members how to view the log in real time and they too increased their batch sizes. At the end of that week the team had their best ever result with a 23 percent improvement. And it was all down to simply asking the Beast to provide the information live.

So by applying the rule The Beast is Alive to the team's everyday task, even though they believed they had gone digital, they discovered a major opportunity that was previously hidden from them. That could just make the difference between Jane being local champion and global champion when it comes to account processing.

> **INSIGHTS**
>
> - Within the capabilities she understood, Jane had done a great job in optimising her performance.
>
> - The original processing speed had effectively been turned down at implementation by using batches of fifty rather than three hundred.
>
> - Both the business and the Beastkeepers had accepted the downgraded performance as normal.
>
> - Jane didn't even know the name of the 'systems guy', so what were the chances of them tackling a problem together?

But smelters are different... aren't they?

That was Steve's response when he heard about the gains made by Jane's team. Steve had been given the job of improving safety in the smelter where he worked, and in his mind Jane's data processing centre was too far removed from his problem. Improving efficiency has nothing to do with improving safety!

'Seven hundred people work here and our safety record is shameful. We really want to improve it. Nobody wants people to get hurt when they come to work. We've had initiative after initiative, each bringing some improvement, but not enough.' Steve's voice trailed away as he looked out his office window to survey an orderly tangle of conveyors, pipes and furnaces stretching across his horizon.

Unlike Jane, Steve had a specific problem to address and he needed to crack it before it cracked him. He couldn't see how rules for harnessing the Beast could possibly help him but at this point any help was welcome. We asked him to explain what was currently being done to improve site safety.

'We conducted a survey earlier this year and we believe we know what's wrong. It is the way we get the shift supervisors to talk about safety incidents with their teams. Or rather the way they don't! We asked them to use the start of each shift briefing to focus on safety. They do it for a while and then it drops away. They say they have nothing new, nothing of interest to tell their teams. We have a daily works report that details all the safety incidents across the site. They agree that this is what they should be using but we can't get it to them on time routinely enough.'

Now that Steve had articulated his problem we could really get to work on it. First we made sure we understood the critical points by restating them.

'Steve, you have seven hundred people whose safety behaviour you are personally charged with helping to change. You believe a critical factor is getting your shift managers to use the recent safety incidents across the site to stimulate their teams to think safety but you don't seem able to get this information to them routinely. Is that right?' Steve nodded, looking even more dejected on hearing the problem described back to him. We asked him to show us where this information comes from and how it is distributed. He sketched the flow of information on the whiteboard, starting with the database where all incidents are recorded immediately after they happen, through the organisational layers, until finally reaching the people who need it most.

Who gets the information and how does it get to them?

As Steve finished, it became clear why the information flow wasn't robust. The information was extracted from the database by Steve's secretary, Charlotte, and put into an email. She always did this as her first job so it could be sent out at 9.00am each day. This email was sent to an extensive distribution list of at least sixty people, covering senior and middle management site wide. Crucially, the shift supervisors were not on Charlotte's distribution list.

'Why isn't Charlotte's email sent to the shift supervisors?'

'We tried it but they get so many emails they don't even look at them until much later in the shift, when they have an hour to sort through them. Now we send it to their managers who print it out and place it in the shift mess rooms. But the managers are so busy that this doesn't always happen. And since the shift supervisors can't rely on receiving it, they stopped using it as the focus of their shift briefings.'

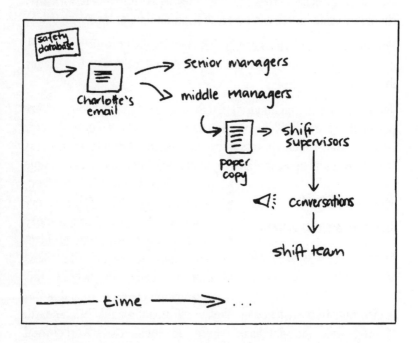

'So if the managers were more consistent with passing the information ...'

'No, that's not the answer.' Steve headed off our query. 'To be honest, even sending it to them at 9.00am is too late. Their shift starts at 6.00am. By the time they get it the information is guaranteed to be twenty-four hours old.'

We looked again at Steve's whiteboard diagram and knew the Beast could help. Firstly, the information was recorded in the Beast's database as soon as the accident happened – no delay. Then the information was extracted by Charlotte and put into an email: some delay developing. And finally, the managers were expected to pass on the information – piling delay upon delay, and adding a major cause of unreliability.

We set about finding a way to cut out the multiple handling of information through layers of management.

'Steve, do all your shift supervisors have access to your company intranet?'

'Of course! That's a company standard. Everyone has access.'

'If we put the information on the intranet, would the supervisors use it?'

'They already access the intranet for union news and other stuff, so yes …' Steve's voice trailed away.

'Can we put it on the intranet?'

'I don't think it'll be easy. The systems people always seem flat out. I can't see that they'll have time to update it each day.'

'What if we explained how important it is?'

'I don't know.' Steve rubbed his chin absently. 'We could give it a go.' He picked up the phone and called Michael, the head of the intranet team. 'A quick question. How difficult is it to get information put on the intranet and regularly updated?'

We watched as Steve listened intently.

'Pretty easy, eh?' He looked surprised and pressed Michael some more. 'Even if we had to update it daily?'

Steve put Michael on speaker-phone so we could listen too and explained the whole problem to him. He pressed the point of how important it was for supervisors to have this information as quickly as possible. When Michael understood the problem in detail he was able to improve on the idea.

'You don't have to even wait for Charlotte's email. We can extract from the database all the incidents occurring over the past twenty-four hours and at 5.45am every day post them on a web page. This can all happen automatically. In fact we can do it every hour just as easily. Then at any point in the day the supervisors will know they have the most up to date information that exists.'

'But the managers will still need the information.' Steve was groping for possible hitches.

Michael laughed. 'Well they can go and get it from the web. That's the beauty of it. Everybody has access to the same information. I call it bureaucracy busting.'

Steve couldn't believe it. His biggest problem, one he had been stressed about for weeks, had been solved in a five minute phone call to a Beastkeeper.

'Why didn't I see this myself? It's so obvious!' Steve stared at us, a look of shame creeping onto his face.

We quickly reassured him by explaining about the Beast. 'It's only obvious if you understand the basic rules for harnessing the Beast. Once you understand them you can apply them to problem solving. And don't worry because you're not alone. Most people haven't changed the way they think about their problems. They don't know about harnessing the Beast. We think it's time for things to change!'

INSIGHTS

- The organisation had made a huge investment in desktop technology but not in training people to think digitally. Steve hadn't changed his assumptions about what was possible and so didn't consider using the Beast to solve his problem.

- Steve's previous solution involved most of the site management, and yet not one of them had suggested using the Beast.

- When we suggested involving the Beastkeepers, Steve's reflexive response was to place it in the 'too hard basket'.

- If Michael truly understood the business impact of harnessing the Beast, he'd be knocking on everyone's doors telling them.

Rule Two Summary

- Information delays can have a massive impact on a business.

- Introducing technology doesn't necessarily remove delays if we keep applying our old thinking instead of digital thinking.

- Even if it looks digital it doesn't mean the Beast is harnessed.

- Only the people working in the business will know the true impact of delays – don't expect the Beastkeepers alone to set up the Beast perfectly for you.

- The Beast is alive, so ask for information when you need it.

Thinking about your Beast

- Make a list of the information you receive each week. Does it simply give you a retrospective view or can you use it to drive your business?

- What ideas do you have that would impact greatly on your situation? What information do you need to make this change? When do you need it?

- What information are you responsible for which may be more helpful to others if it was given to them as soon as it became available to the Beast?

- What key decisions do you make where you don't have the latest information?

- What decisions do you have to wait to make because the information hasn't arrived?

- How much are these decisions worth to you?

The Eco Plastics Story

Although Peter suggested Gus ask Kate to crunch some numbers to test the viability of his waste by-product idea, Gus was reluctant. Kate had already said she thought they shouldn't be 'faffing about' with new product development, so he wasn't convinced she'd do the idea justice. Gus had noticed that Kate was in the habit of using numbers to advance ideas she supports and bludgeoning those she doesn't.

So instead of asking her for a feasibility report on his waste by-product idea, he asked for a profitability report on a job currently in production. Given that she was concerned about too many low margin jobs and too much waste, he chose one that usually creates a lot of waste. Such a high waste product was likely to feed his waste by-product idea and he planned to use the information from Kate's report as a basis for calculating the waste by-product viability.

It was a couple of days before Kate got back to him; she called a management meeting to discuss her findings. There had indeed been excessive waste, so much in fact that the job had cost Eco Plastics money.

'This proves my point about too much low margin work. Unprofitable sales are worse than no sales at all.' Kate waved the report at Peter.

'It's the amount of waste that's making the job unprofitable. It's a production problem. Sort it out Gus.'

'We've been working on that for ages and haven't cracked it. The more we try to solve the problem, the longer the downtime, the less productive we are. It's better to stop selling that product or develop a waste by-product.'

'Stop selling,' said Kate.

'Fix the problem,' Peter countered.

'What about my waste by-product?'

The meeting finished without a clear result. Kate couldn't make Peter stop selling the product, and Peter couldn't make Gus fix the production problem, and Gus quietly resolved to pursue the waste by-product.

That evening he found time to study Kate's report, determined to find a solution. If his waste by-product looked feasible, it was a small step to improving the business's performance.

Based on wastage from this one product, he eventually managed to calculate what the waste by-product would cost to produce. The early numbers suggested it might be viable, but that ultimately depended on the selling price.

The next day he arranged to spend the following Monday on the road with Trevor, their leading salesman, so he could discuss the waste by-product with existing clients. (Although he wasn't planning to call it a waste by-product!)

Gus was growing increasingly optimistic about his project's prospects until Trevor pointed out that there had been another rise in scrap prices. Although the figures in Kate's report were technically accurate, they were now out of date.

The Beast is Mobile

The world is our workplace.
Geography and location are irrelevant.

Boundary-less behaviour allows ideas
to come from anywhere.

Jack Welch

Have you ever noticed the Beast beside you on a plane, or train, or sitting opposite you in another part of your office block? Whether you notice it or not, the Beast is there, brimming with awesome potential. Its agility can improve your processes and its pace can beat your competition to a sale. And the Beast can do all this remotely, even while you're sipping chilled orange juice at 30,000 feet, because the world is our workplace – geography and location are irrelevant.

But you don't have to be crossing borders to benefit from the boundary-busting Beast. Merely by sitting at your desk you can chart new paths for your department and business that were previously considered implausible. The key, as usual, isn't hidden deep within technology, it's hidden in your mind. And the purpose of this chapter is to demonstrate that becoming a digital thinker means also becoming a boundary-buster.

When 'going mobile' isn't thinking mobile

Armed with a mobile phone and a laptop, road warriors and air-mile junkies have been known to roam for weeks before surfacing at their nearest office. These sales people, consultants, service personnel, regional managers and other mobile workers have learned to conduct business from wherever they lay their laptop. But have they taken full advantage of the Beast's mobility?

Sure, they are now carrying far less and roaming for longer; no more heavy trade manuals, catalogues and order books (a benefit for those of us not built like Arnold Schwarzenegger). However, more importantly, as they spend hours on trains, planes and waiting at airports and stations, any variety of business chore can be completed, from writing client reports to preparing presentations to updating budgets and completing staff appraisals. Together, a laptop and a mobile phone function as a mobile office, and the work done on the plane or train can be transferred back to base at any hour, from anywhere. Carrying around a laptop and a mobile phone may make you mobile but it isn't the same as thinking mobile.

Let's talk about Sebastian's experience. Sebastian is one of a number of salespeople who spend three to four weeks every quarter travelling across Argentina, selling crop insurance to farmers. He's been doing this for twenty years, since laptops and mobile phones were mere twinkles in technology's eye, and after all that time has the procedure off pat.

Sebastian meticulously plans for client meetings before leaving his office. He then travels widely, visiting potential and existing clients. On his laptop he carries presentations, additional reading material plus his expense records and client contact information. He is, what most people would consider to be, a mobile worker – visiting clients by day and emailing his office by night – relaying results, questions and additional client contact information. Yet in spite of his experience and organisational skills, things lately have changed for the worse.

Some of the larger, more mainstream insurance agents have started selling agricultural insurance and, although this is new territory for them, they have big brand back up. Some of Sebastian's largest customers have started to waver and the conversion rate of new clients is falling. Previously Sebastian could convert a prospect to a sale with an 80 percent success rate. Now his conversion rates are falling. Some time between meeting with Sebastian and making their decision, the prospect's head is being turned.

Sebastian tried solving this problem by phoning his prospect soon after they received his quote, aiming to answer questions and address concerns before they could become show stoppers. Although this practice proved helpful, it wasn't the ultimate solution. Sebastian knew, with absolute certainty, that face-to-face discussion with the prospect was the only way to halt the slide in sales.

Sebastian took his concerns to Enrico, his Managing Director, who confirmed that this wasn't an isolated problem. Sebastian was relieved to find that the trend was consistent across the sales team and Enrico called a management meeting to tackle it. At that meeting we asked Sebastian to explain his sales process in more detail.

'When I arrive at the client's, we have a chat before getting into the meat of the sale. I find out the sort of crops he's got and confirm the quantity of each. If he's never had crop insurance before I explain how crop insurance is just like any other business insurance, except for farmers their factory is the farm. You wouldn't own a factory without insuring it, would you? If he seems interested I offer to send him a full quote for his crop, insured to the amount of cover he wants.

'At the end of the day I email these details, for each farm I visited, back to the office who email it on to the underwriters, the people who actually take on the risk, in Switzerland. The underwriters normally reply within twenty-four hours and if they agree to take on the insurance they include a quote. Unfortunately most of the farmers don't use email, although this is slowly changing, so we fax and mail the quote to the farmer. This whole process takes no longer than two or three days, but by then I have moved on and am hundreds of miles away, so a face-to-face discussion with the client is out of the question.'

We asked the meeting why the sales team can't give quotations on the spot.

'That's impossible,' said Enrico, shaking his head at our naivety. 'We can't even commit to whether an underwriter will take on the risk. Even though we know the facts – the area and its weather risk status, the quantity of crop and potential value, we simply can't second guess the underwriters, unless we're prepared to take on the risk ourselves; which we're not. It's amazing how often the underwriters surprise us, by either rejecting a case, or proposing a wildly different premium. The only way we'll offer a quote is if we have an underwriter to back it up.'

Sebastian supported Enrico's position. 'There's no way that our underwriters will provide a quote within three hours, so forget about getting one within three minutes in the middle of the night. They already just improved their turnaround time for quotes from two to three days down to twenty-four hours.'

Maria, the Risk Manager, quietly interjected. She deals with the underwriters regularly and explained to the meeting how the underwriters separate policies into two types: cereals and others. Cereals are regular crops that can be quoted on directly, given the location and weather, the crop type and size. However, the non-regular crops such as cotton, require more analysis and decision time by the re-insurer.

'Well that might work for cereals but 75 percent of our clients are cotton clients,' said Enrico.

'Yes, but if we can estimate in advance the information the re-insurers need for the non-regular crops, we could probably get a provisional decision just before a sales meeting.'

Maria's confidence inspired Sebastian. He knew that since he needs to prepare for trips several weeks beforehand, and this preparation includes estimates of farm sizes, crops and locations, he would probably have all the information required. During the sales meeting he could then just firm up the numbers based on the provisional price already provided by the underwriters. If he could be in a position to close deals face-to-face he could significantly improves sales (and bonuses!).

He agreed to help Maria work with the underwriters to see what could be done. He thought it might be possible. After all, increased sales are a clear benefit for the underwriters too.

The underwriters, although cautious at first, could see the mutual benefits and agreed to:

1   Put quotation tables for regular crops such as cereals on a secure website and update them as required. Sebastian would be able to access these tables whenever he needed by using a password.

2   Provide a time-limited quote for each prospect up to one week ahead of a sales call. Within each quote would be a sliding range of charges based on the quantity of crops to be insured in that location. Changes to any open quotations would be emailed directly to Sebastian everyday so he knew the figures were accurate for his meeting. In return, Sebastian would provide the underwriters with crop type, quantity and location estimates one month in advance.

So now all the information that Sebastian would need to provide a quote on the spot was there on his laptop or on the net. Using his mobile phone he could access this immediately, in front of the client and print out a proposal. If the client agreed, he could close the deal on the spot, face-to-face.

The impact of Sebastian being able to spend time with the prospect going through the quotation was significant. By utilising the Beast's power, sales conversions improved by more than 20 percent. Sebastian increased his sales bonus, Enrico's company retained market share and the underwriters increased premium income. And all this was achieved without additional technology investment, just a little applied digital thinking.

So next time you're out and about, take your Beast with you … and make it work!

But my job isn't mobile

Most people work at the same location day in, day out. And if you're one of them you might be tempted to skip to the next rule. However when we say geography and location are irrelevant – we mean it. The fact that you sit at the same desk everyday is irrelevant to the fact that the Beast is mobile.

Let's briefly revisit Sebastian's case study and draw out two important points. Firstly, think of Sebastian's problem without the geography and location. Instead of Sebastian sitting in a remote farm, imagine him simply at a desk in a room. Now put his colleague, who's located in Switzerland, simply at another desk in a different room. Both are sitting in front of connected PCs. Assume the colleague is not always at his desk. Now re-run the problem. Sebastian needs to give a quote to a client who is sitting beside him, while the person who can supply the quote is away from their desk. Isn't this just a normal business scenario?

This reframing of the problem is crucial and can't be over-stated. For Enrico and Sebastian, getting an instant response from a Swiss company in the middle of the night was out of the question. There were just too many issues to overcome: logistical problems, company policies and mental barriers. Yet when their problem was reframed without the geographical content, the solution was considerably easier to develop. Conversely, you may not perceive your job as being mobile yet it still may benefit by getting your Beast to overcome location and geography to perform some boundary-busting.

Thus the second important point to draw from this case study is that once the geographical components have been removed, the problem is essentially one of process. The Beast can readily break time zones and borders, both national and company borders, but doing so requires changes to business processes. No new investment, just a focus on people and how they can best interact to get the output you want. In Sebastian's case that meant quotations on the spot.

By considering location to be irrelevant you can remove mental barriers between you and opportunities in other locations.

Boundary-busting

Another possible way of boundary-busting is reassessing relationships with suppliers.

The supplier in the next town

A chocolate retailer produces seasonal advertising brochures and although their advertising agent is only in the next town, they reduced the turnaround time for getting brochures to market by using the internet and email to view and discuss draft brochures. Decisions are made quicker and the number of face-to-face meetings has been reduced, thus reducing travelling time and costs.

The supplier in the next country

A Sydney based finance company selected a software systems support provider based in New Zealand. Eliminating the mental barrier of location, the company broadened the range of potential service providers which enabled them to find the best fit, rather than merely the closest. The finance company traded expensive technicians on their doorstep for a remote but instant service, whereby the supplier accessed their office systems directly. This enabled the supplier to catch and fix problems earlier than waiting to be alerted to them.

Packing sweets the boundary-busting way

Mike is the team leader for the packing area of a major sweet factory (or as they call it, a *hard confectionery production facility!*). His factory is one of fifty owned by the same large multi-national food producer. His team consists of three shifts with twenty-five people in each.

Mike is responsible for the sweets from when they leave the cooler until they are bagged, packed into cases, placed on pallets and taken away.

Mike's problem, along with the rest of the site management team, is that unless they can collectively reduce the cost per case the factory will be closed. Their average cost for the previous year was about £6.10 per case and their target is £5.30. Everyone has worked really hard over the past three months since learning about the threatened closure and some improvements have been made. The current cost per case is £5.80 but the steady decline has flat-lined and the team is running out of ideas.

Since the packing area is the current bottleneck in the whole sweet making process, Mike has a serious business problem.

Initially Mike's efforts focused on reducing downtime because the bagging machines were losing 30 percent of production time. His engineers identified sealing problems and weight issues as the main culprits and worked hard on these to reduce bagging machine downtime to 18 percent. Even so, Mike's department continued to bottleneck the whole process and Mike was beginning to despair.

We spent time with Mike to understand his issues. His goal was clear, yet his strategy was limited. We asked Mike where the cost figure of £5.30 per case came from.

'From our sister factories around the world. But many of them are in countries where labour is much cheaper. We can't compete.' Mike handed over a report that included his company's worldwide league table for hard confectionery production facilities, pointing out their rank in the bottom half of the list of thirty.

It was clear from the report that the top performing producers were located in Asia and South America, but what was also interesting were the differing rates of production and efficiencies. These varied widely from site to site and we asked Mike how it was possible for these sites to have both higher efficiencies and higher production rates (since Mike believed increased speed meant increased downtime).

'I don't know. They probably run different machinery. Then again, our company has standard suppliers...' Mike was thinking out loud, so we

Why not make a phone call to find out what you don't know?

prompted him to action by suggesting that he call them to find out. Two days later Mike had spoken to ten sites on the list. He was astonished by what he learned. Sure, in some cases there was different machinery, and in others more labour was used or different products made, but many of the sites were simply running the bagging machines faster and at higher efficiencies. Mike was intrigued.

His engineers have always told him that the bagging machines couldn't operate any faster than about eighty bags per minute. But here he was learning about the same machines running at 110 bags per minute. It didn't seem to make sense and his engineers remained sceptical. Mike wasn't convinced either, because the bags were placed in boxes manually so increasing the machines' output would require more packers and therefore increase his labour cost. Just the same, this new information held exciting possibilities and he set about learning more about how it could be applied.

Mike organised a meeting with his engineers for just this purpose. He learned that if they increased the bagging machine speed it would have a knock-on effect; they would also have to adjust the sealer timing, bag forming process and many other variables. Suddenly the amount of information he needed was turning the idea into a cul-de-sac. He had to find information about product varieties, bag sizes, the different bagging machines and whether any modifications had been made to them. And he had to gather this information from a number of people, on a number of sites, spread all over the world – and gather it quickly.

We took Mike to meet his Beastkeepers and got him to explain to Sonia, the IT Manager what he was trying to do. Sonia introduced Mike to their intranet site and showed him a variety of company communities. Each community area shared news, success stories and provided chat pages and download areas.

Sonia was enthusiastic about setting up a community for Mike. 'You provide details of the participants and content and we'll set up the site.'

Mike again got on the phone, calling the company's various sites around the globe and found a keen sponsor in eight of the ten sites he had first spoken with. Together they identified the initial community objectives of sharing machine set-up information, swapping troubleshooting stories and providing a question and answer feedback mechanism.

Within two weeks the participating sites had their set-up information available on their community site for every bagging machine and product. All the information already existed in their respective quality systems so all they had to do was forward the information to the Bagger Community Administrator, who was none other than Mike!

Mike's first win came from a speed trial which was conducted based on information from a packing process half way across the world. The results were exactly as the set-up information predicted. The bagging machines were now operating at 110 bags per minute (up from eighty) with no increase in downtime.

Mike did the maths. An increase in output would require an extra person on each of the five tables packing to enable them to cope. But the increase in output would also allow the line to process their allotted weekly production ten hours ahead of schedule. This meant he could eliminate the current overtime for the thirty-four people working on whole line. So by adding five people to each of the three shifts (3 x 5 x 8 hours = 120 hours of labour), he saved ten hours for the whole line (10 x 34 = 340 hours of labour) and managed a net decrease of 200 labour hours each week.

When we visited Mike a few weeks later the price per case had made a step-wise drop and was still steadily decreasing. It was currently at

£5.43 but Mike was confident of meeting the £5.30 target. And, the Bagger Community Group had blossomed. Many more than the eight initial sites became involved once they saw what information was available. Even the manufacturers of the bagging machines were getting involved. Other areas of the company were pushing for the development of process and machine specific communities based on Mike's best practice site.

Mike was proud of his website and amazed at how easy it had been to make it happen. He confessed to thinking, until he got involved, that these communities were for high tech companies full of computer nerds, not managers like him. Now he knows that a community group is an efficient way of bringing lots of people together who share a common cause or objective, with each member helping the other.

No longer did Mike and his engineering team feel that their packing area was their problem to solve alone. They now had access to the company's experts and resources from around the globe. They continued working through their downtime issues and helping other sites with similar issues.

Mike admitted that although he no longer feared the imminent closure of his site, he was concerned that the cost per case figures across the company were beginning to decline because of the benefits of information sharing. Although Mike's site had moved from the bottom half to the top half in the cost per case rankings, he knew the competition was on!

At first glance Mike would have appeared unlikely to benefit from harnessing his Beast and from thinking mobile. Mike works on a factory site, not even in an office, and he goes to work everyday to the same location. But Mike needed to improve his process. By making geography and location irrelevant Mike tapped into his company's awesome information and knowledge bank and reaped the benefits of live, up to date information that could immediately impact on his team's performance. Mike no longer felt he was battling alone because he had access to counterparts throughout his multi-national company.

The world has truly become Mike's workplace.

A final word on boundary-busting

Another major piece of boundary-busting happened in this chapter – mental boundary-busting, the boundary of responsibility. No doubt Mike believed that it was the Beastkeepers' responsibility to harness the Beast. However, looking at Mike's situation, it is inconceivable to expect that his IT department could have anticipated his needs well enough to identify the solution. Mike crossed that mental boundary and found the solution for himself.

INSIGHTS

- Mike worked at the same location every day and yet breaking the mindset of geography and location was the key to solving his problem.

- Locally, people said increasing the machine speeds couldn't be done. Yet another example of assumptions significantly constraining the business.

- The drive for improvement never stops. In fact it is getting faster and faster. When you make your first major win by pulling the new big lever, don't stop. Keep pulling on that lever and keep scoring the wins.

Transforming Trends

The Beast's power can transform an individual job, a department, a site, a company. It can even transform an entire industry. Take the fashion industry for example.

A simple model of the industry might have haute-couture at the summit, selling individually crafted garments designed for the few. Lower down are the fashion houses, producing high quality garments based on catwalk styles for those who can afford them. Finally, at the bottom end of the market are designers of mass-market garments for the hoi polloi. They too produce garments based on catwalk styles but significantly modified for mass-market appeal and inexpensive production.

These mass-market design houses don't have the money to hire a photographer to attend the Paris catwalk shows. For next season's look they are forced to wait several months for the official catwalk photographers to produce their catwalk exposé. The design houses then use these photographs to generate their own garments. That was then.

Nowadays catwalk shows are revealed at various internet sites on the night of the show. Designers can access these sites directly to generate their next range, thus reducing the product cycle from three to four months to as little as two weeks. This new way of doing business has transformed the industry, giving customers the latest fashions faster and more frequently.

Rule Three Summary

- Once you remove the geographical constraints a problem becomes essentially one of process and people.

- You can go to the same location everyday, yet by becoming a digital thinker you can still enjoy the world as your workplace.

- The Beast is capable of serious boundary-busting – within companies, between companies and across industries.

Thinking about your Beast

- Is there information at other locations within your company that can change your process?

- Are you mentally constraining the way you deal with suppliers or customers (internal or external) by fixating on geography or location?

- Are you waiting for your Beastkeeper to find solutions to problems they don't know you have?

The Eco Plastics Story

Although Gus's rough calculations regarding the viability of his waste by-product had become even rougher because of the increase in scrap prices, he still intended spending a day with Trevor. He reasoned that it was probably a better way of testing the viability of his waste by-product. No market meant no product, and if there was a market, he could assess at what price, and work backwards. Besides, if all else failed, it was good for him to understand another part of the business.

Gus was impressed by Trevor's easy manner with people but alarmed about some of the commitments Trevor was making. They discussed Gus's concerns as they traveled.

'Given the fluctuating scrap prices, how can you be so confident about the prices you're quoting?'

Trevor laughed. 'I'm not as confident as I seem, but who's going to buy from an uncertain salesman?'

'But what happens if you get it wrong?'

'I carry the latest price list. Kate updates it every week.'

'And what if it's wrong when we come to do the job?'

Trevor shrugged. 'That's a problem because if there's too much of a delay between me writing up a job sheet and the scrap being purchased, and the scrap price goes up, then it eats into the sale's profitability. If it's looking too far out I'll try to amend the price by sweetening the pot, promise to bump them up the production queue.'

'Doesn't that annoy the customers though?'

'Sure. That's why we try to carry the loss whenever we can. It's hard competing with the foreign imports. Better not to let them get a foothold.'

By the end of the day, although some customers had expressed interest in his waste by-product, Gus nonetheless felt despondent. He'd gained a better overall picture of the business and therefore a better understanding of Kate's concerns. Not only had he seen first-hand the problems of selling, Trevor had also told him horror stories about the scrap purchasing side of the business.

That night Gus pulled out Kate's monthly reports for the last year. He was no accountant but he pulled out the cash at bank figure from each report. Kate was right – the business was haemorrhaging.

Perhaps she was also right about them not having time to develop new products. Gus decided to park his waste by-product idea and push ahead with his efforts for reducing electricity usage, and therefore costs.

The Beast is Responsive

Feedback and organisational response are instant.

I get an email everyday (on sales data)...
You may see a day where sales spike way
up. I'll call the general manager and say,
'Gosh, what'd you do? Do more of that!'

Jeff Bezos
CEO Amazon.com

Life is getting faster, forcing our decision-making to keep pace. Our customers have more choice and are better informed so they ask more questions. They get restless when answers come slowly, especially if they believe the question should be easy to answer.

We need feedback from our customers as fast as possible. We need to know if they are upset, if we have not met their expectations. If we don't hear and respond to this feedback quickly we will lose them to a competitor.

Just to make it a little more overwhelming, the term 'customers' truly means everyone we interact with, both within our own company and externally. If we are seen internally as a major bottleneck it won't be long before others start asking if it is possible to outsource our piece of the business.

Better have a little lie down; it's tiring just thinking about all these things we have to do fast, fast, fast.

However, there is a limit to how fast people can operate successfully and many are working at that limit. But are we really interacting as efficiently as we could? Are we truly using the Beast to help us? After all, the Beast is meant to work instantly, on many things at once.

Recall from *Rule Two The Beast is Alive* that there's no need to wait for an information post-mortem. So if the Beast can work instantly, the delays are likely caused by our inability to act quickly enough: we don't hear about the problem until it's too late, we are so busy it takes us a week to get around to looking at it and then it turns out to be someone else's issue so we pass it on... and on... by which time the customer is frustrated and dealing with them becomes ever more protracted.

If we can't work any faster, let's work smarter and get our Beasts to work harder.

Quick, answer that call!

'Here we are,' Kim said, opening the door labelled IT Customer Service Centre. 'This is the first floor of our call centre.'

'The first floor?'

'Yes, there are two more floors just like this one, directly above us.' She smiled at my surprise.

We looked around the enormous room full of desks facing each other in circles of five or six. It was an impressive sight. The furniture was modern, the lighting subdued, plants bloomed and water fountains bubbled. It felt like a pleasant place to work, nothing like our preconceived mental pictures of a call centre. We had imagined the office equivalent of a third-world sweatshop, with row upon row of people squashed together in a soul-destroying atmosphere.

Kim continued speaking as we gazed around. 'This is one of only three IT call centres we have in the world to support any issues our 100,000 employees might have. As you can see, it's a fairly new set up, put in only about twelve months ago. A lot of attention was paid to creating a positive work environment.'

Her patter rolled on. She'd obviously conducted this tour before.

'Our other centres are in Singapore and the USA. With us based here in the UK, we divide the time zones in three. Singapore is eight hours ahead of us and we're a further eight hours ahead of Oklahoma City. This means that we can run a follow-the-sun response approach to callers from all over the world.'

'A follow-the-what?'

'That means whatever time of the day or night it might be for you as a caller, we always have one of our call centres operating in daylight hours. That way each call centre can operate at full strength during their daylight hours and only run a skeleton staff overnight. All excess calls overnight are then automatically routed to the call centre where it is daytime.'

'So, a call from the UK might get routed to the Singapore call centre?'

'You've got it. It's saved us millions as a global organisation and significantly reduced our staff turnover rate because the shift patterns are so much more sociable. Of course, it does cause us complications.'

'Such as?'

'When we're the main call centre, we have to be able to answers queries in many different languages. In fact the desk groupings you can see are mainly organised by language.'

Each group of desks had a small flag planted in the centre so that anyone walking past could tell which language they were operating in.

'Fascinating. So what do the call centre operators do?'

'You mean the customer service advisers.' Kim corrected with a practised smile. 'The best way to understand is for me to introduce you to one of the advisers and they can tell you all about it.'

She led us to a group of desks and waited until the adviser finished his call before introducing us. Kim explained that we were visiting the business and she was providing a tour of the call centre.

'Could you take a couple of minutes to show us what you do when answering calls?'

'Sure, no problem. I guess Kim has explained that we handle IT support calls from anywhere in the world and that we are one of three call centres the company operates globally?'

'Yes, she's covered all of that.'

'As you can see, each of us has a phone headset, keypad and PC terminal. Calls are automatically routed to the language group appropriate to where the call is coming from, and joins their queue. I can tell if there are any calls waiting for our group from these lights on my phone keypad.' Darius pointed to a set of three small amber lights. 'When this bottom one is on, there's one caller waiting. If we get two lights, there's between two and five callers. And all three lights mean more than six callers waiting.'

He tapped the keyboard and a blank form came up on the screen. 'When I take a call, I open a call log like this one. I ask the caller for their name and what the problem is, recording it in this form. Our job is not just to record the problem though. We're frontline support so we help the caller fix their problem if we can.'

'What sort of problems do you get?'

'Everything from forgotten passwords to system crashes. There are also a lot of questions about how to do something.' Darius smiled. 'They're the best calls because people are really appreciative when you help them learn something new. They all have access to the online training of course but that doesn't cover everything.'

'So not only do most of the people in this room speak several languages but they also have to know all about fixing PC problems?' The skill level required seemed extremely high.

Darius laughed. 'You do tend to pick up a lot, particularly around the recurrent faults, but we have a cheat sheet.' He clicked an icon on the screen and up popped a search screen. 'We have a database of issues and solutions that has been built up over the last twelve months. If any of us come across a new problem that we couldn't find in the database then we fill in a new database entry and whoever manages to fix it — could be us or could be the tech boffins on the ground floor — fills in the solution. This is available to all the advisers twenty-four hours a day, so it's an easy way for us to share our knowledge.'

'Aha, the ultimate cheat sheet! Do the callers like the service?'

'If you'd asked me six months ago I'd have said yes. But because people are finding our service to be good, the word is spreading and the number of calls is increasing. That means people are being held in the queue for longer and getting very frustrated.'

'Their frustration is understandable. Are there any plans to handle the increase in call numbers?'

'I don't know. I guess all we can do is hire more people to work in the call centre if the call volumes continue to increase.'

As we were speaking the second amber light flashed impatiently.

'I'd better get back to it.' Darius replaced his headset. 'Don't want to make the callers angry. That's no fun for anyone.'

We looked around for Kim, finding her talking to one of the supervisors a few metres away. When she noticed Darius had finished, she came over.

'How did you go?' she asked.

'Darius was great. He explained what he does really clearly. One question though. What are your plans around the increasing call volume?'

'Yes, the number of calls is going up but we've been able to handle the extra calls so far and still keep our performance measures on target. As people find out how helpful our service is they just want more!' Kim rolled her eyes. 'We've got a good team here though and they work hard to record the problems and solutions so that they learn quickly from each other.'

'So your performance measures haven't been affected by the increase in volumes?'

'They have been affected but so far we've managed to keep them within our target range. For instance, the average time callers wait has risen slightly but is still below our ninety second limit.'

'So what other performance measures are critical for the call centre?'

'Time in queue, percentage of calls fixed by frontline support, and average calls handled by each adviser in an hour are the main ones. We also keep close track of staff turnover and skills balance but that's to maintain longer term stability rather than short term performance.' She pointed to a report displayed prominently on the notice board.

We had been walking as we talked and were suddenly back at the door we had entered earlier.

'Well, unless you have any other questions, I think you've seen all there is to see.' Kim efficiently wrapped up her tour.

On route to our next appointment we discussed what we had seen: excellent working environment, efficient recording of issues, good knowledge sharing, measures in place to monitor performance. The call centre seemed to be using technology extremely well to deliver a responsive service. The only concern was around the increasing volume of calls.

'Come in, come in.' Derek smiled and beckoned us into his office. 'Good to meet you.'

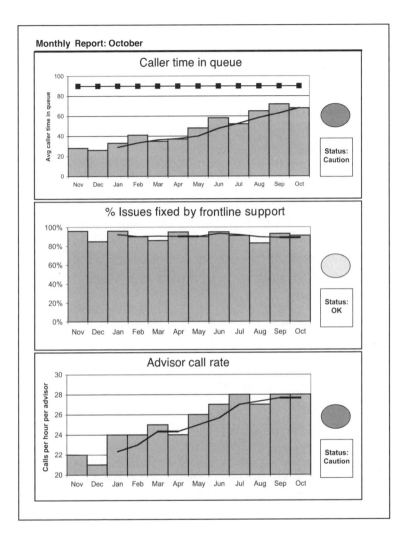

As we settled around his meeting table he asked what we had seen so far and we explained the call centre visit.

'I keep meaning to go over and see what it looks like. They won several awards for the set up apparently. State-of-the-art, as they say. I just haven't found the time yet. We've been so busy.'

Derek was responsible for introducing online training in the organisation.

'The first set of courses that we've taken online is our computing courses. Training on using software packages, accessing the intranet, setting up your PC and so on.'

Derek spent the next fifteen minutes describing the difficulties they had overcome in the development phase: the need for different languages, implementation on different systems, avoiding cultural bias, not to mention the details of content development.

We asked how far he was into the training implementation.

'Oh it's early days in terms of our full training offering because we can deliver any training course in this way, not just the computing ones. However, in terms of the computing courses, the majority have been in place for the last six to nine months. Everyone seems to love them – a great success. So much more convenient than having to attend a classroom session.'

'Moving into online training can be a big cultural change for a company, have there been any problems?'

'Naturally there have been a few issues but nothing too serious. In fact our team has been a lot quieter than I expected. It's going better than I could have hoped.'

'So how do you find out about problems?'

'We have a feedback questionnaire for every online course anybody does. This tells us whether they enjoyed it, found it useful and so on. They're also invited to record any problems they had and it gets sent automatically to our team.'

Derek's response seemed focused on the short-term issue of how well the training was being delivered. His answer hadn't addressed the long-term effectiveness of the training. We went on to describe what we had found earlier in the call centre, about the growing number of calls and particularly, how many of them were not problems so much as learning

How can you best assess your training's effectiveness?

issues. We asked him how he could best assess the effectiveness of the online training and his mood quickly changed. As we spoke, he went from cheerful and proud of his team, to frustrated and angry with the call centre.

'Why hasn't anybody told me! It's no good them just helping people individually and not telling us. How are we supposed to respond to training needs if nobody tells us what's missing? I've got people sitting in my team who can change our courses to eliminate recurrent questions but we're not being told about them.' Derek was a passionate man who cared deeply about what he does. He paced around his office, going red in the face.

After a few minutes of venting, he calmed down. 'There's no point in getting angry about what is already done. The important thing is to get it right from now on. Who was the person you spoke to this morning?'

'Kim. She's one of the team leaders.'

'Let's go and find her.' With that, Derek headed for the door with us trying to keep up. He was determined to sort it out as quickly as possible.

We found Kim and luckily she was between meetings. Derek explained who he was and how, from what he had just learned, there appeared to be an urgent need for him to sit down with Kim.

The objective was clear: optimise the response of the organisation, not just the call centre, to users' issues. They set a time to meet the next day and agreed to cover three points:

1 What information the call centre gathers relating to issues that are training based.

2 How this information might be used by the online training team to implement a root cause fix.

3 How to provide this information routinely.

Within the week the online training team were receiving a weekly, automatically generated email listing the top ten training related issues, with the number of callers affected week by week for the last four weeks. This made it easy for them to prioritise development to ensure they were addressing the most pressing issues.

When we caught up with Derek two months later he was smiling again. 'We were initially shocked at the number of calls but as we started to investigate the top problems, most of them were fairly easy to address. The call centre recorded which users called because of what problem. So we've even been able to go back to callers with a specific problem to ensure we've now addressed their issue. We seem to be getting on top of them quickly. The great thing is we can readily see the result of our changes because we get the call centre information each week. In fact, we could get it each day if we wanted because the system generates the email automatically. But weekly's fine at the moment.'

'So is Kim pleased too?'

'Yes. She says she can see the call volumes starting to drop. In fact she's looking at how they can provide similar information to other parts of the business that are better suited to implement root cause fixes.'

INSIGHTS

- Kim's call centre was responding well to users' calls. Derek's team was responding well to users' feedback on training courses. Each was locally optimising their response. However, the overall response to the organisation's needs was definitely sub-optimised, even though the Beast had all the answers.

- Both Derek and Kim could have identified the opportunity if only they had considered the way the organisation was responding rather than just their team.

Kim and Derek are not alone

If you think the example of Kim and Derek is an isolated case, then think again. Local focus on response to customers is widespread and call centres are frequently a classic example. But why?

Consider for a moment why most call centres are set up: to make customer interaction more efficient. In other words, to reduce costs, make responses more consistent and, largely, to insulate most of the organisation from the troublesome interruptions of customers calling up for help.

Typically, call centres operate almost as a separate department (in fact many organisations have chosen to outsource this service so they're a different company), with enormous focus on the speed of response to a caller – answer fast, deal with the issue fast, take the next call.

Hence the key measures Kim was judged by:

- Caller time in queue (*appear responsive*)
- Percentage of calls fixed by frontline support (*insulate the organisation from the customers*)
- Average calls handled by each adviser in an hour (*or in other words, cost per call*).

Whilst these measures are not in themselves wrong, they drive localised optimisation of response.

If we reframe the role of a call centre, we could view it as the richest source of customer feedback available to an organisation. And what's more, it's all neatly recorded and filed away in an enormous Beast just crying out to be used. Couldn't this be used to solve the underlying problems and not just answer the next call faster?

A supply-chain mesh

Securing a contract to supply home-brand televisions and videos to a major supermarket chain was quite a coup for Bill and George. Now they were a secure link in a supply-chain thanks to a sole importing license arrangement with the producer and a sole supplier contract with the retailer.

Attaining and maintaining the contract meant paying extremely close attention to their relationship with the supermarket management, ensuring their needs were fully met. This was Bill's job and he'd done it supremely well. After only their first year of supply, Bill and George were granted key supplier status in the electrical category.

Achieving this status had not been easy. They had to agree to supply equipment on a sale or return basis for new product trials and take on the whole repair centre activity. This was something the supermarket had previously handled internally.

Bill and George took on a partner to handle the repair side and carefully set up the contract to ensure standard costs of response, depending on the severity of the problem:

- Solving customer queries by phone
- Call out to exchange for new
- Call out and minor repair
- Call out and major repair

These standard charges were applied and billed monthly to the supermarket chain.

The supermarket management loved it. No more troublesome repair centre to run, standard known charges for repairs and a trusted supplier managing the whole thing. Perfect.

George was also focused on the client relationship. His job was to interact with the supermarket's buyers, working with them to determine which products to sell and how many to stock, agreeing wholesale prices and suggested retail price tags.

Everything was going great until the monthly recharge for repairs started to climb and the supermarket management challenged the reliability of the equipment.

This took Bill and George by surprise and in their haste to keep the supermarket relationship strong, their response was to swiftly pass on the complaint to the manufacturer. The manufacturer promised to look into it but in the meantime the situation continued deteriorating.

It was at this point we were introduced to Bill, George and the supermarket supply business. It didn't take long to see what was happening. A total disconnect existed between the importing side of the business which Bill and George ran, and the new repair centre, which was being run by their new partner. (A disconnect also existed at the supermarket chain because its buyers weren't aware of the reliability problem. This meant they were making decisions based solely on the look and specification of the products. They thought they were doing well because product was moving off the shelves.)

Meanwhile the manufacturer had been trying to respond to Bill and George's blanket imperative to 'improve reliability' and conducted a quality audit. However, because they weren't given, and didn't ask for, a list of the specific items that were failing, they failed to identify the problem.

And yet, buried away in the repair centre's Beast was a daily record of which items had the most problems, whether they were serious and what they were costing the supermarket. Enough information existed to seriously improve the bottom line of all three businesses.

When we brought to light the records from the repair centre, it became clear that the top three faults were all related to a single type of television – one of the latest big sellers. Unfortunately, whilst the buyers were overjoyed at how many were selling, the number of repairs was so high that the supermarket chain was actually losing money on the product.

Bill and George, eager to resolve the problem, offered the supermarket management two choices. They could either:

- replace that product with a similar but more reliable one from the same manufacturer, or

- insist the manufacturer solve the reliability problems and keep this product, which customers clearly found attractive.

As the supermarket chain was effectively losing money every time they sold one of these televisions, as well as risking their home-brand reputation, the supermarket management chose the first option. Bill and George arranged for all remaining stock to be returned to the manufacturer.

The repair centre charges immediately fell back to their original levels and the relationship, which had taken so long to cultivate, remained intact.

Of course, Bill and George were keen to avoid similar potential show stoppers and started to produce a repairs report for the supermarket management to accompany the monthly invoice. And, once they got the hang of digital thinking, they went even further and also listed the true margin for each product by taking account of repair costs as well as sales price. Not only did the relationship remain intact but it grew stronger.

INSIGHTS

- The importing business's response was delayed because of the disconnection between the importing and repair functions. This was in spite of the fact that Bill and George remained extremely focused on nurturing the relationship and all the feedback they had received from buyers was positive.

- The supermarket chain's response was delayed because the supermarket management didn't ask for a breakdown of the repairs by product. This delayed the removal of the offending stock from their shelves. The delay meant the supermarket chain both lost money and diminished their home-brand reputation.

- The manufacturer's response was delayed for the same reason. This meant it continued shipping faulty products all over the world.

- Meanwhile, the repair centre was making money. So no reason existed for it to alter the status quo.

Responding to external customers

The case studies presented here highlight situations where the secondary or internal response to a problem was failing. We selected these examples because, in our experience, they represented the response opportunities currently being missed.

In fact, over the last ten years, organisations have put a great deal of effort into using the Beast to tackle the first-line response to external customers. Whilst some have the wrong drivers in place and so provide a fast but poor long-term solution, there are many ways that the Beast is being used well. A few examples are:

- Highlighting unusual usage patterns to tackle ATM and credit card fraud.

- Providing shipping details on the web to allow tracking of a parcel and likely delivery date.

- Preventing 'stock-out' by automatically increasing the stock of items that start to sell fast.

- Suggesting book titles you may enjoy based on your previous buying habits at online bookstores.

Rule Four Summary

- In many businesses the Beast is already hard at work providing a fast, first-line response to customers.

- Having a good first-line response does not mean that the organisation is responsive.

- The Beast frequently holds large quantities of data that will allow major improvements in secondary or internal responsiveness.

- A delayed response can, in the short term be financially

costly, and cause long term image damage to a carefully nurtured brand.

Thinking about your Beast

- Every business has the opportunity to buy technology to create a fast, first-line response. As this is now so prevalent, doing so only allows you to keep up with the pack. The real business advantage comes from using this fantastic untapped source of power to revolutionise the response of the whole organisation. Aim for quick, fast and appropriate.

- Is your business gathering major customer or product feedback yet only partially responding?

- Has your business made the most of the Beast in ways that are now becoming commonplace such as automatic flagging patterns or abnormal changes?

CASE STUDY — CASE STUDY — CASE STUDY

The Eco Plastics Story

Gus was on the phone to a manufacturer of electricity monitoring equipment when Neil, the scrap buyer, walked into his office. Gus could tell by his expression that it wasn't good news.

Gus quickly finished his call. 'What's the problem?'

'We don't have enough scrap to run this afternoon's job.' Neil held his hands up, palms forward. 'It's not my fault. Peter's got the sales boys all revved up. They're making the sales but not keeping up with the paperwork.'

'Okay. What can you do for me?'

'Your boys have just finished the set up. That's how we found out there wasn't enough scrap for the full job. You can either split the run, and do another job in between, or redo the set up for the next job. Your call.'

'Either way I lose production time.' Gus wandered out to his scheduling board with Neil following.

'There's another problem too.'

'Go on.'

'We won't meet the delivery date Trevor promised.' Neil again offered his palms for examination. 'Sorry Gus. Like I said though, not my doing.'

'Are we okay for the rest?' Gus waved at the schedule board. 'I need to know I can juggle freely.'

'Yeah. No problem. If you plan to finish Trevor's job tomorrow, I'll make sure the scrap's here.'

Gus rang Trevor to find out if the customer would accept a part delivery on time, and the balance a day later. He knew it was inefficient to make two deliveries but was mindful of Trevor's concerns about not letting the competition get a foothold.

The customer agreed and while the first part of the job was running Gus rearranged his schedule board, juggling delivery dates and slotting jobs in to maximise any possible economies of scale.

There was no way around it though. On top of the double delivery of Trevor's job, it was going to cost him in overtime to make up for setting up twice.

The Beast is Empowering

Better business decisions are made with greater confidence.

Bad decisions are the result of guessing.

Michael Hammer

Once upon a time, business decisions were regularly made from experience and gut instinct. Even if the data existed, information just wasn't as readily available. Then in the 1980's, along came spreadsheets, such as Lotus 1-2-3, data became more manageable and business decisions became propped up by graphs and tables. Suddenly it became impossible to imagine a manager's life without a spreadsheet program and it's been that way for twenty years.

Now it's possible to power business decisions using the Beast because, not only is more data gathered, it is easier to manipulate and analyse.

Of course, as stated in *Rule One*, all information is accessible so more opportunities can be seen. But how is the Beast empowering?

Empowering means authorising or enabling individuals to take action or make a decision and the impetus to take action is based on the interplay of three key factors:

> **Size of the prize**
> **Certainty of success**
> **Cost of failure**

It follows then that the greater the **size of the prize**, the more inclined you will be to take action. The prize, or benefit, may be a positive outcome or the removal of an anticipated negative outcome. Therefore a benefit could be increased sales (positive) or solving a problem that threatens the closure of your department (the removal of a negative). However, the benefit has to be sufficiently rewarding to motivate action, so it is important to understand the size, and therefore value, of an intended action. The Beast is empowering because it can help you put a value against your prize.

The next impetus to take action revolves around the **certainty of success** – the greater the certainty, the greater the impetus. Even when the prize is large, if the certainty of success is small, the impetus is neutralised. If your action is unlikely to increase sales or prevent the closure of your department then you are, quite rightly, unlikely to take that action. However, too often little certainty exists because people don't know how to assess certainty and not because certainty cannot be ascertained. Unfortunately, the default position is uncertainty, and this paralyses action: Inaction is deemed better than the wrong action. The Beast is empowering because it can help you better assess the certainty of success.

Finally, there is the **cost of failure**. If you take action and it fails, there is a cost – money, time, respect, career prospects, pride. You could argue that when people buy lottery tickets the prize is large and the certainty of success small, which suggests that people won't buy lottery tickets. However, the missing part of the equation is the cost of failure and in the case of buying a lottery ticket, the cost is spare change – no loss of respect or pride or career prospects. However, even when the cost of failure is great, by using the Beast to increase your certainty of success, you are more confident to take that risk.

Most inaction occurs because people are either unaware of how large the prize is, uncertain that their actions will yield the desired result, or calculate that the cost of failure is too great. The Beast is the best way of providing these answers and therefore empowering you to make better business decisions with greater confidence.

Empowerment is even greater when anchored to the other rules for harnessing the Beast. Most strategic decisions are made by managers standing above the process, rather than from within. This causes delays and distortions. However, if information is available to everyone who needs it (Rule One), and available live (Rule Two), anywhere, anytime (Rule Three) then to enable instant feedback and organisational response (Rule Four), more people need to be empowered to take action.

People with the benefit of local knowledge, making hundreds of small decisions, can dramatically impact on the success of a business unit. However, it is irresponsible to simply authorise people to take actions and make decisions without first enabling them to make informed decisions, certain of their results and their prizes. So give your people more than the right to make decisions, give them the information they need to make good decisions.

Let's take a look at this in action.

Milking the cash cow

Angela is the CEO of a large North American distributor supplying yeast and yeast extracts, mainly to the baking industry. She has worked in the business for over twenty years as the company expanded into most states and Canada. Her company is now a mature cash cow, generating good profits with little new investment required – so the theory goes… and more importantly, what the shareholders are expecting.

When we met Angela she was stomping on her management team. Profits had been declining for the past five years – not massively, but steadily. Shareholders were fidgeting and pointing nervous fingers towards Angela. Costs were static with most of the warehouses and vehicles now fully depreciated. Sales had risen with the market and their market share remained steady but average margins were creeping down, causing declining profits.

The management team were despondent. The Financial Controller thought that the financial system needed to be upgraded. He believed it didn't provide the kind of up to date margin information they needed and he even doubted whether the current cost model was right.

Rick, the Sales and Marketing Manager, had succeeded in maintaining market share in an increasingly competitive environment. He didn't believe any more could be expected from him. After all, it was a mature sales market with long term bakeries buying from trusted suppliers. There weren't many new bakeries setting up each year and when they did, Rick's people were snatching the lion's share of the business. To all intents and purposes his team was doing the best they could.

Angela sighed. She wanted to start thinking out of the box but most of her ideas meant more investment and she knew that the shareholders would balk: cash cows were meant for milking not fattening. With this in mind she agreed for us to see whether her Beast could unlock any opportunities.

First stop was Rick's department. He gave us a run-down of how things worked.

'We have over thirty sales people across all states. Obviously their sales performance varies, but overall we have a good set of experienced people. We sell various grades and types of yeast. Normally, if our client needs our products, we are the sole vendor, but sometimes a customer will use multiple vendors for different products. On top of sales work, the team collects information on all customers; existing and potential. So we have a comprehensive database of our market share.'

We took to the road and followed one of the recommended sales people, Jimmy, around for a few days, visiting existing and potential customers. For all new sales he consulted his price list on a spreadsheet. Often a customer might want to negotiate a deal. When this happened Jimmy called back to the office to get Rick's approval.

After one such negotiation we spoke with Jimmy.

'You can understand my main aim is to get the sale, to clinch the deal. It's very frustrating for me if Rick doesn't give me the go-ahead for a deal. It puts a real dampener on any further sales negotiation. The customer often feels they're dealing with the hired help and would rather bypass me altogether. It's hard to get back on an equal footing and the sale is often lost. Since my bonus is tied to sales revenue, I can't say I like the process much, and to be honest I don't think the customer does either.'

Back at the office Rick explained what he did during a negotiation.

'During a negotiation I consult our finance system to get the latest margin information for the products being negotiated. If it looks like the margin is too small, I block the sale. I know the team doesn't like this much but if we let too many low margin sales go through our company profits will plummet. If it weren't for me those sales folks would send us out of business. All they want is volume, volume, volume!'

We raised the idea with Rick of giving the sales team the information they needed to negotiate. They could each have access to the listing of

Why not give the sales team the information they need to negotiate?

costs, recommended sales price and margin for each product, and do the negotiating themselves. Rick leaned back, sucking air through his teeth. 'That's just not the way we've done business in the past. It's putting a lot of responsibility on our sales staff and, to be frank, I don't think it will improve the sales revenue or the profits.'

'It probably won't,' we agreed, 'so long as their bonus is tied to revenue. But if this is shifted to profit, things might change considerably.'

The idea was presented to the sales team at the next monthly meeting where mixed feelings were aired. Many of the older sales people weren't keen at all. Although it would grant them more power and responsibility, their bonus income might change considerably. A few of the younger sales people were intrigued to see the margin information for the products, so a listing was produced. This caused more than a little commotion.

One of the junior sales people said that had she known these figures, she could have increased the profits on a sale from the previous week.

'Arco Bakeries wanted a lot of our prime yeast. There were three choices and based on their dough mix I suggested one that would do the trick – KS42, a mid-priced yeast. I knew it looked good to them, since it was mid-priced, and at the same time would generate a good revenue for us with the volumes they wanted. Now I can see that had I sold them KS20, a slightly less expensive, but less potent product, we could have significantly increased the total profit of the sale. In fact…' she reached for a calculator and did a few sums, 'we could have increased the profit on that sale by 30 percent.'

The room erupted as sales people pawed through the product figures. This was enough to convince most of them that it was worth trying but the issue of the bonuses would have to be addressed quickly. And this investigation turned into a bombshell.

They graphed each sales person's figures for the previous year, alongside the profit generated.

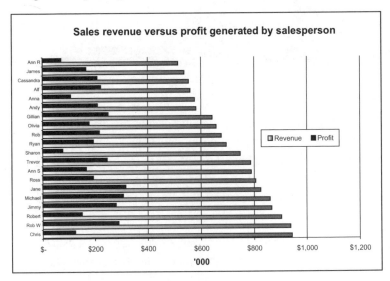

A massive difference existed between the two. Some sales people were top on the revenue sales list but mid-field or lower on the profit list. And some, who had always been considered poor performers because of their low revenue figures, had fantastic profit figures.

Even more insightful was the combination of the profit figures and the market data the sales people had gathered. A map was drawn up for each state showing existing and potential profits. In this way a sales efficiency number could be generated. For example in Texas, Jimmy's state, he generated $334,000 in profit the previous year, from a potential of $1.7 million. Therefore he was 20 percent efficient in capturing the profit market from his state.

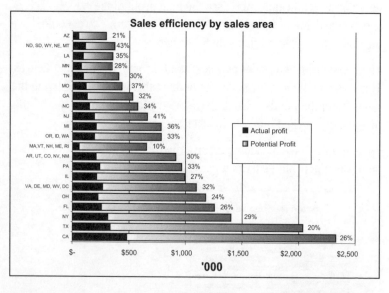

By doing this for each state, all the sales people could see how effective they were at garnering the opportunity within their area. Obviously market share was one component that makes up this efficiency but the other component was the price at which they sell their products. They could now see two very important and distinct levers for their business rather than one.

The results were tremendous. First of all, the sales team asked for a client listing ranked by potential profits, rather than potential sales.

This alone meant they spent more time focused on customers that could yield greater profit. The state efficiency graphs led to changes in the sales territories so that more people could work in areas of higher profit potential. And of course, armed with the margin information, the sales people could do most of the negotiating themselves. They built a simple spreadsheet listing all the products with the margin information next to each. By setting the proposed volume and sales price for each product the client wanted, they could see the total profit that would be generated from the sale. By raising some prices, lowering others and substituting different products they could put together deals that both pleased the customers and generated greatly increased profits.

Once the bonus system changed from revenue to profit the company saw a jump in monthly profitability, and two quarters later, they had increased overall company profitability by more than 20 percent. Not all the sales people worked well with the new system, for example those that didn't want the responsibility, or those that relied on selling lower cost product or reducing prices to win the sale. This wasn't easy for Rick, but ultimately if the company wanted to survive it needed sales people who could generate profitable sales.

Angela was more than a little emotional about the results. 'We didn't spend one more cent on capital, yet my profits are now heading in the right direction. And you tell me it's all because of the Beast in my company!'

We used the Beast in many ways. By giving the sales team access to the Beast's information they immediately spotted opportunities to improve their sales and increase company profits. Combining information from different parts of the Beast, the market information with the margin information, meant turning the sales model on its head. The model was no longer focused on sales revenue, but rather on company profits.

This created a tremor of panic as company policies and ways of doing business were tested. This is what the Beast is all about. The Beast gives you new ways of tackling old problems but you must be willing to reconsider policies set before the Beast was harnessed. However, once people could see the benefits, there was no turning back and now the sales people increasingly rely on the Beast to tell them about their customers, their sales areas, their efficiencies, and how to put together win-win deals.

The size of the prize

Rick was reluctant to empower his team to make individual decisions. He doubted it would improve revenue or profits. However, by consulting their Beast they learned that the size of the prize was much larger than they had guessed. In Jimmy's area alone the prize was valued at over $1.5 million (potential profit minus current profit).

For the individual, the knowledge that they were performing well below potential profit removed all uncertainty about the success of changing the bonus system from revenue-based to profit-based.

The costs of failing were simply loss of sales and/or sales personnel where the new approach didn't work for them. With the prize so large and the downside of inactivity so great, this cost was acceptable.

INSIGHTS

- The bonus scheme was set up to drive volume, which is good when you're trying to capture market share. However, in a mature market, where positions were well established, it completely failed to drive sales correctly.

- The guesswork had already been taken out of the deal-making process by checking margin information. However, old business practices meant that only Rick held this information. He hadn't used it to empower the sales people at all.

- The Financial Controller assumed the financial system needed upgrading. He wanted to spend more on his Beast when in fact, it was being under-utilised and thinking proved to be the big lever.

Crisp action

With the Group General Manager visiting in two days to see how he was settling in, Jeff wanted to make a good impression. Jeff knew that if problems continued in the current pattern, there was an excellent chance of the Group General Manager arriving to find the plant at a standstill. Jeff strove to balance the pressure of the upcoming visit with taking the time to make the right decisions. What he didn't know was that this situation would seriously test his leadership ability and it was only his second week with the company.

Jeff had just taken up a new appointment as plant manager at a potato crisp factory. During his first shift meeting Jeff noted that the crisp line efficiency had dropped over the past month from an average 92 percent to 85 percent. There were various regular problems but the new issue was around the waste water pump. Over the past few days the pump had stopped, on average, for over four hours every day causing the whole line to cease production. Jeff was keen to ensure this problem was solved quickly and decided to demonstrate to his new team the type of decisive action he expected from them.

He started by asking Louis, his Engineering Manager, to explain where the troublesome pump was involved in the process.

Louis explained how the potatoes arrive on trucks and are loaded into hoppers that drop the potatoes into cleaning drums. These drums wash the potatoes with water to clean off any dirt and debris. The waste water pump removes the soiled waste water from the cleaning drums. When it breaks down, the drains flood, and the whole operation stops.

Jeff asked Louis what he thought was causing the problem.

'It's that whole waste water pump system. It was designed poorly from the start and now it's really showing.' Louis was quick to point out to his new boss that it was done before his time. 'The whole system needs replacing. I'm chasing up quotes for the work right now.'

Next stop was the Production Manager. Katrina had been in the job for several years and was more than a little stressed. She was cursing maintenance when Jeff arrived.

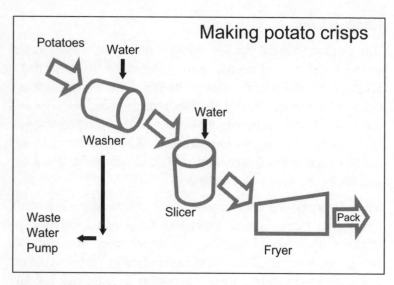

Jeff asked her what was going on.

'It's that rotten pump. It tripped again. It's completely knackered. Why don't they replace it instead of calling in the mechanic? There was a similar problem last year and we ended up replacing the pump. That fixed it then, so why don't we do the same now?'

'I heard that Katrina!' It was the mechanic jumping to his own defence. 'It's not our pump. It's your new operators. They push too many potatoes into the cleaners and overload the pump. Too much dirt goes through and clogs the filters. I've told them about it before but …'

'There's nothing wrong with our new operators. They've been well trained and you shouldn't be telling them what to do anyway. If you think you have a problem with one of my team you should come to me first.' Katrina was beginning to overheat.

How long has the problem been occurring?

Jeff jumped in, firmly insisting that fighting amongst themselves would not help solve the problem. He guessed that the blame-shifting was probably due to them being as keen as he was to make a good first impression but it wasn't helping. He calmly explained that collectively they needed to get to the bottom of the problem soon, and asked them how long the problem had been going on for. Katrina was first to respond. 'A few weeks, I think. You can find out exactly from the downtime logs in the shift supervisor's office.'

Jeff wandered down to the office but paused by one of the more senior operators waiting by the peeling station for the line to restart. Jeff introduced himself. The operator's name was Gretel and she re-iterated some of Katrina's thoughts. Gretel volunteered that she had trained some of the new operators. She agreed some of the night-shift operators had received less training and might sometimes allow too many potatoes into the cleaning drum but she thought this was rare. Jeff asked her what she thought was causing the problem.

'I think it's the potatoes. Now and again we get a bad batch and the machines go haywire.'

Jeff moved on to the shift supervisor's office to look at the downtime sheets. As he was shuffling through them Ivan, one of the clerical staff whose job it was to enter the data, leaned over and offered to pull a report off the system if Jeff wanted something specific.

Jeff asked for the waste water pump downtime for the past week by shift. Within a moment Ivan obliged.

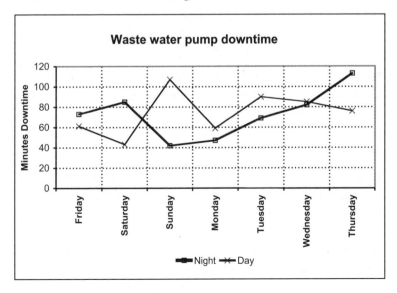

The downtime had been fairly consistent across shifts and he thought back to all the causes that each person he spoke with had suggested.

- Louis said it was the poor design of the waste water system.

- Katrina thought the pump needed replacing.

- The mechanic said the new recruits were overloading the water drum.

- Gretel thought it was a bad patch of potatoes.

The downtime report only enabled Jeff to rule out one of these ideas. Although the timing of the problem coincided with the arrival of the new recruits, he was satisfied that they weren't to blame. The report showed that the downtime was consistent across all shifts and inconsistent with the shift placement of the recruits.

That left Jeff pondering three possible causes. He could see no easy way of verifying whether it was the poor design of the waste water system so he put that idea aside for the time being. The pump may need replacing but ordinarily they last more than a year and Katrina said it was replaced only twelve months ago. If it does need replacing then what could be causing the extra wear and tear? Gretel blamed the potatoes and Jeff dismissed this as a classic example of blaming the raw materials. He'd heard it all before: no matter what the product or the plant, whenever the source of a problem was difficult to pin down, people blamed the raw materials.

Meanwhile, time was ticking by and the Group General Manager was due in two days. Jeff felt no closer to solving the problem. His team, although keen to help, all had their own ideas, all different, yet none proven. He decided to use the data system to dig further and look at the waste water downtime to trace the start of the problem.

It was clear from this graph that the problem had started promptly on Thursday of week twenty. Interesting... if it was the design of the waste water system, why would it suddenly start to cause this downtime unless something in the system had broken? As for the pump wearing out – once again, why wouldn't this happen over time rather than in one day? And what about the potatoes? It's possible.

Jeff thought he could eliminate the potatoes quickly by finding out if the batch changed on this date. Once again Ivan was the man for the job and within moments he pulled the supplier data from the MRP (Materials Requirement Planning) system. The batch of potatoes had changed on that day, but then again, they changed quite regularly.

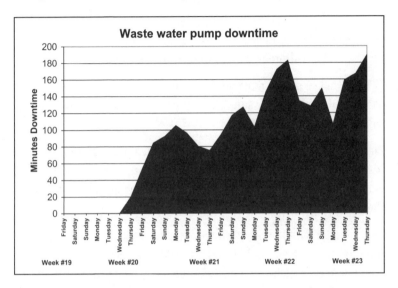

'Ivan, can you pull off the pump downtime data going back a few years?' Jeff asked, and within a few minutes the following graph appeared.

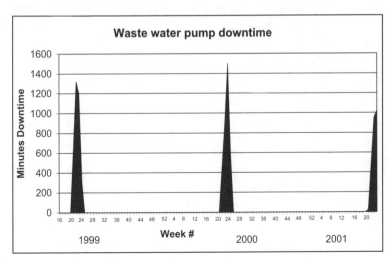

Amazing! A problem appeared roughly the same time every year for the past two years. This looked like more than coincidence. He again accessed the system to check the supplier information and found out that the same supplier provided these potatoes at that time each year. Things were starting to add up. But what could be the problem with these potatoes?

Jeff went out and sheepishly showed the graph to Gretel. After all, in his own mind he had pretty quickly fobbed off her potato idea.

'Well it makes sense, that's the only supplier who grows potatoes in sandy, rather than clay, soil. The sand must be the problem,' Gretel said, when she saw the graph.

Louis was brought in and agreed immediately that the sand doesn't dissolve in the water like the clay soil. This meant that it could accumulate at the filter and eventually restrict the flow of water and trip the pump.

Next time the pump went down they opened up the filter box to find it full of sand. Problem understood. Now they just needed to work out a solution. It didn't take too long for Louis to come up with a routine for changing the filters on a regular basis until they could find an alternative source of potatoes. To Jeff's delight, he not only had the line up and running for the Group General Manager's visit but he earned the respect of his staff.

The impetus to act

Jeff's prize was the respect of his staff and Group General Manager, along with the saving of the downtime costs. The value of respect to Jeff was immeasurable. However, had he wanted to, he could have accessed the system to calculate what all the downtime had cost the company.

For Jeff the cost of failing was great too. Taking the wrong action could cost him personally, by losing the respect of his people. However, there was also a large business cost in the cost of continued, prolonged downtime, plus the additional costs associated with the wrong decision

`– misspending on a new waste water system, new pump, or new training procedures.

Jeff needed to make a decision quickly and with a high degree of certainty because the cost of inaction or incorrect action was too great. By supplying the information, Jeff's Beast empowered him by increasing the certainty of success and thus enabling him to make a better business decision with greater confidence.

INSIGHTS

- The pump had been replaced the previous year at a cost of £10,000. Everyone believed this had solved the problem but in fact it had merely coincided with the end of the sandy batch of potatoes.

- The organisation had empowered Jeff to take action. He could have asked for the pump to be replaced, increased training for the recruits or even agreed to a costly redesign of the waste water system. But it was the Beast that empowered Jeff to take the right action.

Putting a value on the prize

The key to estimating the size of the prize is to put a value against it. As an added bonus, putting a value against a prize also provides the key to prioritising action, making it easier to determine where efforts are best directed. The following are two diverse examples of the importance of valuing the prize.

Soggy biscuits

In a biscuit factory, a manager from a different area noticed that a large number of biscuits were constantly being rejected at the end of the oven. When he spoke with the operator on the fifty metre long oven, he was told that this was normal and most of the biscuits were out of specification on moisture content. The manager spoke with accounts, got the price of a biscuit and then worked out the average price of a bin of waste biscuits. He then calculated the value of one bin of waste per day for a year, and repeated this for two to ten bins of waste. It turned out that the oven operator typically wasted at least seven bins every day, costing the company £140,000 a year. As soon as the operator saw the size of the problem he set about forcing a solution. This was all the impetus he needed to take action.

Previously, although the operator believed the moisture problems were due to burners that didn't work, he could never prove it and Maintenance wouldn't act on his theory because there were hundreds of burners; finding the ones that did or didn't work would take them days. However, since the size of the problem was valued at such a high amount, the maintenance team could no longer avoid the issue. They put in an application to purchase a Scorpion – a device that goes into the oven at one end, passes through with the biscuits, recording temperatures along the way which are then viewed on a computer screen. Fortunately during the application process, it was realised that the company already owned a Scorpion, purchased earlier by the R&D Department. (A classic example of technology being under-utilised!)

When the Scorpion was used in the production oven the results revealed cold spots throughout. This certainty was all that Maintenance needed to check the burners in the relevant areas. Almost a third of the oven's burners were found to be faulty. This not only saved most of the out of specification biscuits but enabled the oven to be run at a higher rate of throughput, since its speed had been constrained because at higher rates the moisture content in the biscuits rose beyond the specification's limit.

So not only was the waste reduced, saving £140,000 a year, but the throughput increase of 5 percent resulted in a further £100,000 annual saving.

Windows of opportunity

A large multi-national company faced the daunting task of migrating 120,000 PCs worldwide from Microsoft's Windows NT to Windows

2000. It had eighteen months to accomplish this.

Step one involved moving individual user computer accounts including log-on details, personal home drive data, local settings such as browser favourites etc, along with changing the physical PC. This changeover was staggered by region over the project period.

Step two, the migration of shared data, hit a snag at the planning stage. Company policy deemed that, for security and data management reasons, nobody with an account in the old environment could access data in the new environment. The proposed solution, therefore, was to run the old and new servers in parallel until all accounts accessing that data had been migrated.

However, whilst the bulk of users for a given shared drive were usually local, the global nature of the company meant that some users were situated elsewhere. Due to the staggered regional migration, these users may not yet have had their accounts migrated. In fact, geographic access for any particular shared data would likely follow a bell curve.

This meant that parallel servers would be run to service a very small minority in the tail of the bell curve.

Everyone agreed that it seemed excessive to run parallel servers to satisfy relatively few users. However, along with the company policy regarding data security, there was another policy, that everyone should have access to the information they need (Rule One The Beast is Accessible). Consequently, nobody considered other options. Company policies were effectively barriers to thinking.

When these policies were challenged, it became apparent that the policy dealing with the security issue was out of date. It was based on the fact that in the past the systems weren't capable of managing the security. And although the Beastkeepers knew that it was technically possible with the current systems, they were responding to a business policy, and just assumed that it was still valid.

Still, the Beastkeepers had to be pushed beyond this constraining assumption, and so a quick calculation was done:

3,000 servers worldwide
Assume an eight-week delay (conservative)
US$1,274 per week industry standard costing for running a
server
Impact
= 3,000 x 8 x US$1,274
= US$30million (one off cost during project).

Suddenly everyone was interested and consequently, a solution was readily found. A consensus was reached to manually manage the security of the last 5 percent of users on shared data drives, thereby allowing the migration of the shared drive without the estimated eight-week delay. The value of the prize was sufficiently rewarding to motivate action.

The Beast is empowering for you

Use the Beast to gather information about the size and worth of taking action. Then use it to confirm that your actions will yield the desired result. Once armed with this proof, getting people to follow and help you will be easy. People are happy to help if they know they will have an impact, that their cause is important and that their actions will yield results. Otherwise, without these two elements, getting people to help you is based on your relationship with that person and the time they have available.

The Beast is empowering for others

Empowering people to make better business decisions is morale-boosting for them and rewarding for managers. As more decisions are delegated, more time and energy is available for managers to consider more strategic decisions. Should you have any doubt about delegating decision making, you can use the Beast to assess such an action in terms of the size of the prize, the certainty of success, and the cost of failure!

Rule Five Summary

- The impetus to act depends on the size of the prize, the certainty of success and the cost of failing.

- Giving people the authority to make decisions requires also giving them the information to make good decisions.

- Putting a value on the prize drives and prioritises action.

Thinking about your Beast

- Consider a major decision you are facing:

  - How can you put a value on the prize?

  - What is your certainty of success for action options?

  - What is the cost of failing?

- How often do you delay or fail to take action because you haven't gathered the evidence you need to be confident of success?

- How many decisions made in your organisation each day do you think are based on hunches, 'experience' or guesswork, when the evidence already exists? How many of these decisions might be incorrect?

The Eco Plastics Story

'The figures still make grim reading.' Kate passed around the monthly report.

Peter immediately slipped his copy into a folder. 'I've got loads of work in the pipeline. Next month's report will show we've turned the corner.'

Gus found the cash at hand figure. It was down again.

Kate continued, 'That's all very well if they are profitable jobs but I think Gus and I proved that not all of them are.'

'If you're referring to that one high wastage job, then all you've proved is that we need to reduce our waste.'

'But last month's figures show an increase in labour costs.' Kate stabbed at her report. Gus cringed; he didn't want to get into a blame session about the overtime.

'That's the problem with you bean counters, always nervously looking over your shoulder. I've been doing this for twenty-five years. It's all about volume. The more you sell, the more money you make. It's that simple.'

Kate spat back, 'We need to reduce costs to be more profitable. It's that simple.'

'Speaking of costs,' Gus jumped in, trying to take the heat out of the argument, 'electricity is one of our major expenses, along with labour and raw materials.'

'I'm glad you mention labour costs. We should move to a four day week as quickly as possible,' said Kate.

'You can't just cut peoples' incomes by 20 percent,' snapped Peter.

'Better than cutting it by 100 percent.'

'I've looked at the various products on the market.' Gus passed a brochure to Peter. 'This one's the best value.'

'What's this?' Peter stared at the brochure that had suddenly appeared in his hand.

'It's for monitoring our electricity usage. Remember I said that it's unexpectedly shot up by 15 percent?'

Kate jumped in before Peter could respond. 'I've had a look at the electricity invoices. Our annual outgoing is £150,000. Even if you manage to reduce it by 10 percent, it would only be a saving of £15,000.'

'Even less once you've bought this thing.' Peter handed the brochure back to Gus.

'It's a start.' Gus's voice cracked. He was tired of having his ideas shouted down without a decent hearing.

'It's not the solution.' Peter's words were said kindly enough but Gus was beyond soothing.

'Well it's better than your pump up the volume strategy. More like pump up the unprofitable jobs. It's playing havoc with the scheduling and the sales team is making promises that I have to deliver on. I've had to pay overtime to keep on top.' He saw Kate about to react to his overtime confession, and cut her off. 'I bet that isn't accounted for in your average cost per unit figures.'

Neither Peter nor Kate had ever seen Gus lose his cool.

The Beast Communicates

Effective communication is easy.

Yadda-yadda-yadda.

Jerry Seinfeld

Most people agree that communication is a good thing in business. We hear a lot about communicating to ensure business goals are clearly understood by everyone within the organisation. We're committed to communicating with our customers, our suppliers, and our shareholders. We can communicate in person or via videoconference, use the landline or satellite phone, fax, text or email. The mantra is: communicate, communicate, communicate. Yadda-yadda-yadda.

We're all doing it, lots of it. But is it effective? With all this communicating going on, are we missing the message? Are we communicating for communication's sake?

Communication is not effective when we start each working day with fifty emails unopened in our inbox. It's not easy when we're communicating so much there's not enough time left to do our jobs well. Communicating isn't effective when much of it is indiscriminate. It's better to communicate clearly and efficiently rather than in volume.

The Beast provides multiple avenues for communicating easily but it's up to us to choose and use these avenues appropriately. The important task is to recognise the different options and create a communication strategy rather than taking one, such as email, and inappropriately using it for everything.

Used appropriately and effectively, the Beast makes communication with others easy.

Talk takes time

William failed to turn up to our Saturday golf meet for the third successive week. This time when he called to cancel he also asked for help. After getting him to describe his problem over the phone, we agreed to pay him a visit.

William said he felt as though he was *running in quicksand*. His company had recently 'resized to match future needs' which meant middle managers like William were doing more with less. We knew him to be a very competent individual but now he was feeling overloaded by the demands on his time and, as friends, we were keen to help him out. Often it needs an impartial outsider's view to provide a fresh perspective.

'Let's make this as brief as possible so as not to worsen your situation. What are the things you have to do, and let's see if there are any ways to help?'

William opened his diary to a neatly organised 'To Do' list. 'I've always been a really organised bloke,' he stated as a matter of fact. 'I've done all the time management bits. I've categorised by urgency and importance, stripped away all the tasks that weren't important and put the non-urgent ones on hold. But I'm still left with more than I can manage. If I can't find a way to get through it all then I'll just have to suggest getting a second person in to share the load. That won't go down well though because we've just cut 30 percent of the workforce.'

'So these items on your list are those remaining after you've stripped away the unimportant tasks?'

'That's right. I'll take you through them.'

He started to explain the first point but the phone rang, interrupting him. William answered it, flashing us a *See what I mean* look.

'It's Greg,' he whispered, covering the mouthpiece with his hand. 'He runs the equivalent of my division in the South. Won't be a minute.' William listened patiently.

'Look Greg, I've got some people with me right now. Can I call you back with that update in an hour or so?' He paused. 'Yep. Promise to give you all the details. Your meeting's at eleven right? I'll make sure it's before then.'

William replaced the receiver, turning on the answer-phone as he did. 'Sorry guys. Didn't mean to be rude. That's a good example of what I'm talking about though. Now, since the resizing, we're all encouraged, or rather required, to network with our peers. Good idea, just takes a lot of time for little immediate benefit. Greg wants an update on the project we're doing so that he can talk about it at his department meeting today. They're thinking of doing something similar. I'll call him back after we're finished but that'll be another thirty minutes gone.' He smiled, shook his head and added *Call Greg* to his list.

'Right, where were we? Ah, the trimmed down, really-truly 'Must Do' list.' Even under pressure, William managed to retain his sense of humour.

He started talking us through each item on his list:

1 Write up and distribute minutes from last week's department meeting. ('If I don't get these done this morning they won't be ready before the next meeting, this afternoon.')

2 Prepare for meeting at headquarters tomorrow; plane tickets, taxi, notes from previous meeting. ('I could really do without this. It'll

take all day for a two hour meeting and it's twice a month now, *to encourage better communication and common goals.*')

3 Complete quarterly performance appraisals for Gillian and Irene. ('These are already late. It's not fair on them. I don't mean to let them down. I just need some quiet time to complete them properly.')

That's as far as he got before there was a knock at the door. William looked up, his focus on the list interrupted abruptly. It was Ben, his boss.

'Hi Will.' Ben smiled broadly as he came in uninvited. 'Sorry, didn't realise you were busy.'

William introduced us, explaining that we specialised in helping businesses make the most of their existing technology.

'Great – always keen to find new ways of improving.' Ben turned away from us to address William again. 'Just thought I'd drop in to see how things are going. Everything okay I trust?'

'Yes. Fine thanks,' William lied, telling Ben just what he wanted to hear.

'So how's the new project going? The leadership team were asking me yesterday and I promised to get an update from you. Can we catch up straight after lunch?'

'Well, yes, I suppose so.'

Ben seemed to miss the reticence in William's voice. 'See you in my office later then.' Ben turned and, with a nod in our direction, disappeared – along with another thirty minutes of William's day.

'Look guys, I'm going to have to press on and get these minutes done now.' His apologetic shrug told us the situation.

'That's okay William. We've got a picture of the problem. Did you arrange for us to see your IT guy as we asked?'

'Seamus said you could call by any time this morning. I'll point you in the right direction. Can we meet up for an early lunch?'

When we met William in the canteen two hours later, his day hadn't improved.

'The morning's gone and I haven't done half the things I'd planned. I know it's important to talk to each of these people but I have to get my work done too.' He forced a smile and asked how we got on with Seamus.

We explained that we had needed to speak with Seamus to understand just what technology infrastructure the company had available. It turned out to be a typical large company infrastructure with PCs on every desk, common data servers, an intranet and high speed network tying it all together.

'What do you think? Can you help?'

'We can certainly help you to use the Beast to take on some of your workload.'

'The what?' He laughed and shook his head. 'And I thought I had troubles. You're mad! What are you talking about?'

We briefly explained the Beast, sketching a quick illustration. He laughed again. 'Looks like a friendly enough fella. You've cheered me up just by describing him. But how can he help?'

'Most of your day appears to be spent communicating to people in some way or another. The Beast is particularly good at certain types of communication. If you can offload these bits, it'll free you up to have the conversations that only you can have.'

'Example!' He demanded, copying one of his favourite characters from Pulp Fiction.

How much of your time is spent answering the same questions?

'Let's consider two ways the Beast communicates really well. Firstly, the Beast is excellent at communicating the same information to several people all at once. Particularly if they each want to receive it at times that suit them.

Secondly, the Beast is an expert at long distance communication.' William was nodding his understanding but it was time to bring it home to his specific situation. 'How much of your time this week will be spent answering the same kinds of questions asked by many different people, or travelling to meetings?'

William thought for a moment. 'A lot I guess. Perhaps 40 percent.'

'So if the Beast can put a serious dent in that 40 percent it'd free some time for you to do the things nobody can help you with.'

'Sure, saving 20 percent gives me back a whole day every week. But I still don't see how.'

We mapped out alternatives to the way William was currently spending his time, focusing on just three specific actions:

1 Write a brief project update each Friday. Post it on the web and accompany it with a Frequently Asked Questions (FAQs) section. This would cover the majority of information people like Ben and Greg needed to keep them informed. Even if they come back for further discussion, it would mean not wasting valuable time simply going over the facts. Expected return: five hours weekly.

2 Attend every second meeting at Headquarters via videoconference. Expected return: six hours fortnightly or three hours weekly.

3 Key the department meeting minutes directly into a laptop during the meeting. Agree them at the end of the meeting and place them on a shared network drive, ensuring attendees have access immediately. The minutes will be more accurate too, ensuring no need for extra emails bouncing around to make modifications. Expected return: one hour weekly.

William brightened. 'Is this all possible?'

'So Seamus says. He didn't see any problems at all. In fact, he's keen to help you set it up and said you should call him.'

'I will, straight after my meeting with Ben.'

William had a spring in his step a couple of weeks later. Seamus had set up the project update site with the FAQs, the videoconference booking was in place for every other Wednesday, and the direct input of the minutes was going smoothly.

'It's working brilliantly and I'm amazed how easy the changes were to implement. The videoconferencing suite was hardly ever used, everyone's commented that they're getting better informed on the project, and lack of action following department meetings can no longer be blamed on a lack of minutes. In fact, we've come up with some new ideas to help us communicate as a project team…' William went on enthusiastically, well on his way to becoming a digital thinker.

The excessive email conundrum

One of the ideas William and his team came up with was directed at combating excessive emailing. William had to wade through fifty emails every day because everyone routinely copied him in on their communications. Sure, the Beast makes communicating easy but William decided to make it efficient too. A lot of the emails he received were for his information only and, although he needed access to the information, he didn't need to have his own copy.

Enlisting Seamus's help once more, William set up a bulletin board for his team to post the sort of information that he, and others, could access when, and if, required. For some team-members it took some time to break old habits. However, whenever William was copied in on an email that would have been better placed on the bulletin board, he simply replied with a word of encouragement to do just that. His team soon learned to discriminate how they best communicate using the Beast.

INSIGHTS

- The organisation's push for peer networking was translated as a need for more one-on-one verbal communication. Whilst talking is critical, it isn't always the most effective way and should be viewed as part of, rather than the whole, communication process.

- William applied all tactics he knew to prioritise his time and yet this was still not enough.

- The lack of use of the videoconferencing suite was indicative of the company's unharnessed Beast.

Speed up by speaking up

When you're already one of the country's largest plastic bag makers and still can't fight off international imports, you start to wonder whether it's time to pack your bags. When you're the Managing Director, this decision weighs heavily and relentlessly.

Casey had been Managing Director for the past three years, during which time he had implemented many of the things that the textbooks told him to do.

'First of all, we decided that the only way to compete was to become one of the biggest players and benefit from the economies of scale. We set about buying up all the small players. We made seven different deals and grew our market share from 26 percent to 47 percent.'

The increase sounded positive yet Casey's expression remained negative.

'It wasn't a happy period. Let's face it. The only reason for buying up the competition was to radically cut fixed costs and most of the fixed cost in our business is labour. We sacked 30 percent of the combined workforce and relocated all the businesses to this one, purpose built site.'

'That must have had a positive impact on your fixed costs?'

'Of course, but when you account for the cost of borrowing to buy the businesses, the reduction in fixed costs hasn't been enough. We still can't compete with the imports on price.'

'How are you trying to further improve profitability?'

'Over the past year we've rationalised our product offering. In our business, that means focusing only on the major clients. Our main customers are the national supermarkets who require large numbers of plastic bags year in year out. The smaller orders to local shops and small chains are just not profitable for us, so we've backed away from these contract renewals. However, right now we're pitching for a contract renewal with our largest customer. We were very confident until we got wind of the competition.'

'And the competition is from imports?'

'They're the serious competition. There are others pitching too, but typically small players who won't be able to satisfy the consistent high level of quality and delivery that the major supermarkets demand. I'm not worried about them. The imports from China however are a serious threat. They have a proven track record of high volume production and delivery and can offer a price significantly below ours.'

'So price is the major difference between you and the imports?'

'Yes. Our customer says they'd rather go with us because we're based in this country. They try to source locally wherever possible, but say the price differential this time is too much. Unless we can drop our price, we won't get the contract and that'll be 25 percent of our volume out the door – another nail in our coffin.'

'What would have to change to enable you to meet the price challenge on this contract?'

'We believe we've got all the big hits in fixed cost reduction, so the only option left is to significantly improve the output rate at which we make bags. If we could make more bags every day with the same equipment and number of people, then we'd reduce the unit cost of production and so be able to sell more.'

Casey explained how they knew that there was variation in the rates of production. For proof, he pulled out the weekly management report showing how the output varied from day-to-day. He went on to explain that they had been trying to improve the overall output for several weeks without success.

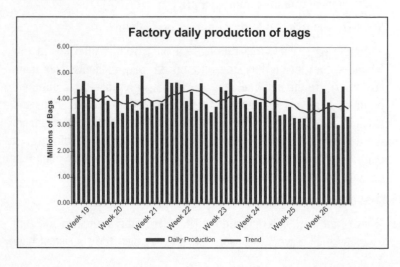

'We've told the shift supervisors how critical this is but we just get told all the reasons why it can't be changed. They say it's just part of the process – some bags run faster than others and some days they all run slow! They reckon the equipment isn't up to the job.'

'If the production rate is the only key lever left, we'd better take a closer look. Who can show us the production process?'

'Billy's your man. He's the supervisor on day shift. You'll find him on the factory floor, can't miss him. Ask anyone.'

We left Casey worrying about losing his largest customer and set off in search of Billy. Sure enough, Casey was right, everyone knew Billy and he was easy to spot at 6'6", topped with a shock of bright red hair. Imposing as he was, he proved to be a gentle giant and more than happy to show us around once we'd explained our conversation with Casey.

The factory was just a large warehouse type building with forty machines lined up on both sides of a central walkway. The machines were all similar although not identical.

'Basically, what you see here is a collection of the best machines from all the factories we amalgamated when we moved to this site. They all make plastic bags, so are fundamentally the same but the machines are made by several different manufacturers,' Billy explained.

We started to discuss the specific problem of output rate and Billy explained that, because of the range of both machines and bags, it was very much up to the experience of the operator as to what they judged to be the optimum run speed.

'At the start of each shift, every operator is assigned a machine and a production schedule for the day. They all know we need to produce as much as possible and they're left to set up and run as they see best. Most of the operators are pretty good but I know some are less experienced and probably don't squeeze as much out of the machines as is possible. But what can I do? I can't babysit them all, not with this many machines and products to supervise.'

Billy's point was fair enough and the major blocker seemed to be the variety of machines and products, along with a range of operator experience. We wondered how much of the variation was due to operators not knowing optimum run speeds for each machine/product combination.

'Billy, where do you keep the records of the product runs and outputs achieved?'

'At the end of each shift it's all put into our production system.' Billy took us into his office and showed us the production system. It recorded all the product runs each day, specifying by operator, the machine used, quantity produced and wastage.

'Billy, what we want to do is work out the value of run speed variations because, if it's significant, it'll be worth working out how to help the operators achieve the optimum every time.'

We selected a high volume product that Billy knew they ran frequently and used the system's report builder to select the output per hour for every run of this product over the last six months. Billy said they always ran this product on four identical machines, so all the runs should be comparable. The results surprised Billy. 'Well I never. I had no idea the variation was so great.'

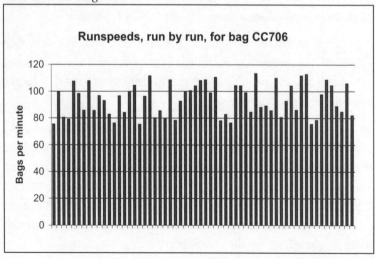

The best run had been 115 bags per minute (bpm), whereas the average was only 95bpm — a difference of over 20 percent. We checked a couple of other high volume products and found similar results. Clearly opportunity existed here, if only the high level of output could be achieved routinely. After a quick calculation of unit cost, it looked like a 10 percent improvement in the high volume products would allow Casey to reach the price point he needed to secure the new contract.

'It's nearly the end of shift,' Billy said. 'It's not a good time to talk to the operators. How about we speak to them all at the start of shift meeting and see what they say about this.'

The meeting with the operators was interesting. Billy was careful to make clear that no one was being blamed for poor performance, phrasing it that the aim was to explore how optimum output might be achieved to secure the much needed contract.

The operators were aware of the company's situation and concerned for the future of their jobs and the business.

Angelo summed up the general feeling well. 'We're all doing our best but there are so many products, with different materials, different prints and different machines — it's not surprising they don't run consistently. And with the pressure on to produce as much as possible every shift, we no longer have time to talk about the best way to do things. Even our weekly Best Practice meeting has fallen by the wayside.'

How can we ensure key information is successfully communicated?

A chorus of muttered agreement echoed Angelo's concerns. Clearly they were all individually doing their best but felt hamstrung by a lack of opportunity to benefit from sharing their experience and information. We needed to find a way of recording and sharing optimum run speeds for all the combinations of machine and product runs, and the relevant set up details required to achieve these optimum runs. We asked the shift for their ideas on ensuring this key information is successfully shared.

It was clear that a collective desire existed to improve and we discussed ways of getting the optimum run speeds from the few to everyone. Eventually a list developed of what was needed:

- Find out what the best output rates had been for each machine/product combination over the last six months.

- Use this data to set targets for each run.

- Get the operators who achieved these best runs to record the set up details.

- Issue this information to operators at the start of a run and update it as further improvements were found.

The obvious next question was how to manage all this information.

'No problem,' beamed Billy. 'The production system can hold all that information and print it out on the daily schedule sheets. It's just that we've never bothered filling in those fields. It never seemed worth the trouble.'

There was a buzz amongst the operators as they left to start their shift. Billy promised to have the target rates compiled by the end of the day for each of the products scheduled to run over the next week. He also agreed to allow whoever had achieved those best rates to help in the set up and record what they did.

The next day Billy lived up to his word and against each daily schedule was a target output rate. The set up was still blank of course, but the box was ready to be filled in that day.

Billy was excited but nervous. 'I sure hope this works. The targets for today are all well above the averages. This is so important, I'm holding my breath and crossing my fingers.'

Billy need not have been concerned. Of course, there were initially a few questions and misunderstandings concerning this new way of working but in the main, the shift kicked off smoothly. Billy spent the day going around each operator, checking how things were going, encouraging them to push harder for the targets, and congratulating them when they were succeeding. Even so, at the end of the shift Billy remained nervous.

'We won't know for sure until we see the numbers,' he said. 'Ned's entering them now. Should be about ten minutes.'

Ned printed off the results from that shift, together with the target and average numbers calculated the day before. The step change was remarkable. All products had run above the average, with about half achieving or surpassing the target. Billy danced a little jig.

'Brilliant result!' he exclaimed, finally considering it safe to exhale. He studied the list carefully, hardly daring to believe what he saw. 'Casey needs to see this. He needs to see it now.'

Billy jumped up and marched towards Casey's office. Casey seemed taken aback to see the enormous Billy charging into his office at a time when most people had left for the day. Billy's joyous mood soon dispelled any fears he might have had.

'We got 8 percent today but I think we should be able to hit 15 percent.' Billy slapped the list of numbers down in front of Casey.

'Billy, what are you talking about?'

'Sorry. I guess I haven't explained myself.' Billy sat down and talked Casey through the achievements of the last twenty-four hours.

Casey's initial scepticism was no match for Billy's enthusiasm. But Casey's immediate interest was in finding out what this meant to the price he could offer in the new contract. He punched at his calculator. 'We need about 11 percent Billy. Do you think we can get it?'

Billy beamed. 'I reckon we can boss. Leave it with me.'

Billy was true to his word and over the next three weeks the operators managed an average increase of 14 percent in output across all products. This result was achieved simply by communicating what a few people knew to all the others who needed to know.

Three weeks later Billy was still stepping lightly. 'What's more amazing is that the improvement hasn't stopped. Of course, we're not step changing every week like we did early on but everybody's trying to find new ways of improving on the targets. It's become a game for the operators and injected a lot of fun into every shift. Whenever someone hits on an improvement, we immediately update the system so every future run benefits from the new information. It has dramatically altered the atmosphere on the floor. Everyone feels like the future is more secure.'

INSIGHTS

- By using the existing system to manage and communicate best practice, the operators step-changed the performance.

- Information on output rates, previously only available in management reports, now drives the actions of those who influence output.

- All the knowledge existed in people's heads but wasn't being communicated to those who could benefit.

- Casey did win the new contract and went on growing the business by competing for contracts that they previously had no chance of winning.

- Weekly Best Practice discussions were an inappropriate communication strategy because with the wide variety of machines and products, the topic each week was only relevant to a few people and even then, maybe not immediately. As it did not give immediate results, it fell by the wayside when the pressure was on.

Rule Six Summary

- The Beast makes communicating easy but because it is so easy, it can be misused.

- In the first case study there was too much communication and in the second, too little. It is better to focus on effective communication.

- The Beast's communication ability is much more than email.

- Effective communication means using the most appropriate medium, combining web pages, phone, email, videoconference and face-to-face.

Thinking about your Beast

- Consider a major piece of communication that you deliver each week. Are you using the most appropriate medium or combination of media to deliver this?

- Where does information remain solely in people's heads, potentially causing sub-optimisation as well as frequent calls on the information holder's time?

- How much time could you save by effectively offloading communication to your Beast?

The Eco Plastics Story

Gus's outburst at the last directors' meeting shocked them all but none more than Gus himself. It had become normal for Peter and Kate to clash but Gus was always the calm one. Losing his temper had frightened them all so much that they agreed they needed to find a way of working better together. Gus tried to remember the last thing they all agreed on but his thoughts were interrupted by rising voices outside his office.

'What's going on?' He had to yell to be heard above Trevor and Jack's shouted argument.

'He's bumping my jobs,' Jack got in first.

'I promised my customer this job would be delivered by Thursday.'

'It's not my fault you missed your spot in the queue.'

'I didn't miss my spot. My job was sold before yours.'

'Let's sort it out calmly.' Gus ushered them into his office so they could sit down. He listened to each in turn and then promised to get back to them after he'd spoken with Peter and Kate. He knew that the choices were to pay overtime to meet both delivery deadlines or let one customer down. It was a lose/lose situation and he wasn't prepared to carry the decision by himself, not after the last directors' meeting.

Gus found Kate and filled her in on the situation as they walked to Peter's office. He'd made up his mind to let them fight it out between themselves but they were surprisingly subdued.

'Can't we just run the largest job or satisfy the biggest customer?' Kate asked, without any conviction.

'How much overtime are we talking about?' Peter asked Gus.

'A couple of hours.'

Peter looked at Kate but she merely shrugged. He then looked down at his desk, at nothing in particular, and said, 'run the overtime.'

It occurred to Gus that although they were working together, the end result wasn't necessarily any better.

The Beast is Efficient

Data is captured and stored once.

---

60 percent of personal assistants believe their boss would make the entire business more efficient by becoming more proficient with a computer.

Office Angels and
Microsoft Research 2002

Jason works away from home every week. Every week he stays at the same hotel, and every week they ask him to fill in his details. Responding to a letter from his car service centre, Ricardo phones to book in his car only to be asked to provide his name, address and car registration number – again. Eileen opens a letter from her bank offering her the chance to benefit from their new service, simply by filling in the enclosed form, which starts by asking her to fill in her name and address.

Every week Jason's hotel reminds him that his weekday abode is no home away from home. In spite of being a regular guest, Jason doesn't feel any warmth in the hotel's welcome. Ricardo wonders just how well his car is being looked after when the service centre is doing such a shoddy job of managing their information. Irritated, he decides to find another service centre. Eileen just couldn't be bothered. She drops the form in the bin and doesn't give it another thought.

If your business is repeatedly asking for the same data, it's a sure sign your Beast is out of shape, fat and unproductive. And the chances are you don't even know. But your customers know, and it will be affecting your business.

However, there are people within your business who do know. These are the people whose job it is to collect this redundant information. They may know because they feel the snap of customer backlash or hear the moans and sighs that follow every request for them to *fill in their details*. They may know because it is a really, really boring part of their job. They may know because they have to sort out problems that arise when multiple records produce inconsistencies due to data entry errors or incomplete updating.

The reason that you don't know could be because these people feel that they're not paid to improve the business, or believe it's not their place to tell you how to do your job. Or perhaps they've mentioned it but nobody listened, or perhaps someone listened but didn't consider it worth tackling. Think back to Rule Five and Jeff with his waste water pump problem. It was the operator who rightly suggested the potatoes as the cause, yet Jeff's first response was dismissive. Recall too the £140,000 worth of rejected soggy biscuits. It was the operator who correctly identified faulty oven burners as the reason.

Maybe you do already know because people are turning up to meetings with conflicting information, bogging the meeting down with discussion over the accuracy of reports or arguing over who owns the right to the latest data. All this time is 100 percent non-productive, non-value adding time, on top of the wasted time in multiple data collections. Consider Jason's hotel. Filling in the details takes just a minute and then another two minutes to enter it into their Beast. If we assume that fifty people check in daily, of whom half are returning guests, then every day twenty-five minutes of guest time is wasted, and fifty minutes of staff time. An hour and a quarter daily, nearly nine hours weekly, 450 hours a year that could be spent productively. (And we haven't even begun to calculate the cost of aggravation caused to both customers and staff.)

Since Rule One was applied, information became available to everyone who needed it. With Rule Two humming along, information is available live, so existing data should not have to be re-captured. Rule Three ensured that no matter our location, we can access the information we need. Rule Four created a responsive Beast and Rule Five made it possible for individuals to make better decisions by valuing the prize. Finally, Rule Six made sure that everyone is communicating, so ideas should be flowing. In theory then, Rule Seven should be redundant. However, let's look at the following case study to see just how easy it is to overlook data duplication problems in all guises, and therefore why this issue merits a separate rule.

Fresh outlook

Mel was excited about her new job as administrator at a publishing company. She was taking over from Rob who explained it was a painstaking job and hugely iterative. For the next five months, most of Mel's job was setting up the project meetings for fifteen teams of editors, over 150 people, for the whole of next year. Rob admitted he was relieved to be passing the job onto her.

The first step in the process was to send a paper memo to each department head. By looking at last year's memos, Mel could see who had received the memo, their role and which meetings they were responsible for. Mel adjusted last year's memo and sent it out. The memo asked department heads to tick boxes indicating whether they would be running the same meetings as last year, to specify their team-members and list any new projects requiring meetings.

Mel then set about organising the meetings. First she printed out sheets of weeks from the diary on her PC (Microsoft Outlook®). Then she identified three alternative meeting slots throughout the year and emailed these possibilities to each team member. Unfortunately, each person kept their own diary with their own meetings, so many of the proposed slots were already unavailable. For added complexity, some people were team-members of multiple departments, so booking them into meetings proved impossible without their managers' intervention. This procedure bounced back and forth for weeks until finally the meeting dates were settled and Mel manually blocked these dates on the printed calendar sheets.

The last step in the process was to book the meeting rooms. Although Mel held most of the meeting room books, some were held by other administrators. This meant phoning each of them to request availability. The process was long and laborious, with numerous changes and frustrated administrators and an even more frustrated Mel. After five months of spending over 60 percent of her time on this process, Mel was no longer excited about her job. In fact, she was determined to change the process or change jobs.

Can the IT system solve my problem?

Mel was adamant that there had to be a better way. The major problem was that two sets of diaries were being used (individual ones and the set Mel used), as well as multiple meeting room books held by a disparate group of administrators. The only hitch was that she didn't know what the Beast was capable of, so she approached the large IT department and asked them if the IT system could solve her problem.

She was told that the person doing her job years earlier had already got them to build a central diary system and mail merge set up for the memos, which saved that administrator months of manual work. They didn't seem happy revisiting the issue but remained helpful.

Mike, one of the Beastkeepers said, 'The whole reason we set the system up was to speed the process of meeting setting for the administrator. By centralising the diary she could use last year's diary to kick off this year's, so she would be halfway done.'

'This seems good in theory,' blurted Mel, 'but lots of changes occur between last year and this year and even worse is that each person has their own diary which I can't see. This means I have to come up with three or four combinations of meetings for each team and even then it often gets rejected.'

'They've all got Microsoft Outlook sitting on their desks. The easiest thing in the world would be if they used Outlook's calendars. Then you could see all team-members' availabilities at once. We suggested this a few years ago but all the editors seemed dead against having Outlook forced on them. So that was that. Our job isn't to question the business. They're our customers. We can only do so much, even if the way they choose to do it appears silly.'

Mel was flabbergasted. This solution, having just one set of diaries, sounded as if it would solve the biggest part of her problem. She thanked Mike and went back to speak to some of the department heads. She found that many didn't care one way or the other and a few were already using the Outlook programme. However, some reported a kick back from their team-members so Mel went to speak with the team-members mentioned. Initially their preference was to use book diaries. However, when Mel showed them the Outlook diaries they became interested, although remained scared. The bottom of the issue was that they hadn't used the Outlook diary, didn't know how and were nervous.

On her way to speak with her manager, Mel bumped into Mike. He called out, 'Hey Mel, I forgot to mention that we could also set up your meeting rooms with diaries as well. That way you could check availability and make bookings at the same time. Would that be any use?'

'Fantastic!' Mel said, knowing as she did that it would entail a diplomatic effort to wrest control away from the various current diary owners.

In the meantime, Mel reported her findings to her manager, Sabiha, who proved surprisingly dismissive. She remained unconvinced about forcing the whole unit to use Outlook and disinterested in Mel's pleas.

What was going on? Mel couldn't believe her ears. After getting so far, she couldn't believe it was going to get blocked. But why? Instead of quitting, Mel became more and more motivated to get this change done. It was the most sensible thing to do, not just for her, but also the company as well. She just had to think of reasons why it might be good for Sabiha.

Mel was asking the organisation to change the way they did business, yet she wasn't providing them with strong enough reasons. She decided to speak with Kate, the accountant, and together they worked out the savings from using the proposed process. Mel spent a few sessions with Kate, who was happy to help create a proposal for reducing costs, and spent more time with Mike to see exactly how it would work. Everybody in the team had a networked PC with Outlook, which they were already using for email, so their Beast definitely possessed the power. She drew up the new process, finalised the proposition with Kate and sat down again with Sabiha.

Sabiha was taken completely by surprise. She hadn't realised the costs, both personal and financial. By changing the process, Mel could do her work in just four to six weeks instead of thirteen to fifteen weeks. It also reduced the editors' load and ensured that the meetings were diarised correctly the first time. This meant that for every team meetings would be scheduled before the new year began, rather than three months into it. It also meant that Mel could take on some of the workload of the other administrators. Sabiha could either reduce the amount of temp hours or try passing on more of the editors' load to the administrators, freeing them up to do even more editing. She was starting to see the benefits. The only cost was some initial training for those who didn't feel they could use the existing diary program on their PC.

The new process was a raging success. The following year Mel completed the entire process in just over four weeks. The few dissenting editors received training, leaving only a handful still against the electronic diaries but who used them nonetheless. Sabiha was amazed and her area won an internal company award for business excellence. She was over the moon.

All it took was a question: *How can I get the existing system to solve my problem?* In this instance it was getting the Beast to be more efficient and getting individuals to use one diary that everyone can access. Data, a person's diary, was now collected at source and available for everyone else, including the administrators (consistent with *Rule One The Beast is Accessible*). Another positive side effect was that now everyone could book meetings with other people by looking at their diary first. Not only was it better for Mel, but for all the employees.

Whipping the Beast into shape isn't always a pushover, especially when it crosses organisational boundaries, both internal and external. Most people believe this is because of technical reasons: the systems can't do it, or it's too hard, or too expensive. This is because business people often don't understand their Beast's capabilities (see Part Three *Recognising the Divide*). In fact, it's the organisational change, the change to people's work that is most often the greatest obstacle.

Once people are comfortable with the way they do things, they are loath to change. You can't blame them. It often takes a long time to get everything under control. In cases like these, it's imperative that the benefit of the change is crystal clear, especially to the decision makers. And remember that benefits aren't always financial. In the case we just looked at, getting the meeting schedule done before Christmas was a huge benefit for Sabiha and made her look good to the rest of the company. Other categories of benefit to consider are: greater control, improved timing, increased morale, greater environmental compliance, safer working conditions, better customer service and improved product quality. By prefacing your solution with the benefits, the decision maker is better able to decide whether or not the solution you are proposing is worth the pain of change.

> **INSIGHTS**
>
> - The capability to radically improve the meeting co-ordination was already in place (the financial investment had been made). It was cultural, and not technical, issues that had prevented the benefits from being realised.
>
> - Even when Mel detailed the solution, she still couldn't convince people to change until she put a value against the benefit.
>
> - Mel was not the first person to try to fix this problem and it wasn't the first time the Beastkeepers had been involved.

Asian crisis

Maya ran a tight ship. She was the Indian Office Manager for a global telecommunications company that had moved into India five years ago. She was recruited at start-up and had grown the office to around seventy people. Her staff was comprised mostly of sales and administrative people. When we met Maya, she was pouring through spreadsheets and printed financial reports. Now and again we would hear her mutter under her breath 'ahh cha chaa', the very Indian response to almost any situation.

'I've checked it and double checked it and I'm sure I'm getting overcharged for training.' Maya took us through her scrupulously well-ordered spreadsheet of training activities for each person in her office. It listed all her employees and all the training modules they had undergone. In addition, it priced each training module and kept a mirror page of costs by month for the past five years.

'This isn't the first time this has happened,' Maya said, 'I've chatted with my counterparts in Thailand and Malaysia. They are all experiencing similar problems. Many of them weren't keeping records like me but after they became suspicious about some of their charges they put together their own spreadsheets to track their training costs. It's not just training either, a few months ago the Indonesian office manager received an unusually high recruiting charge and later found out that he had been charged for a person they had never even recruited! Who knows what they're doing in Finance. I'd better give them another call. It's all such a waste of time.'

Finance was located in the regional head office in Singapore and happened to be our next port of call.

Across a broad desk sat Scott, an expat Financial Controller overseeing the South-East Asia region, who confessed, 'this has been going on for years now. I can't blame Jeanne, the Human Resources manager. She inherited the mess from her predecessor twelve months ago. It's got a little better, but it still costs the organisation at least a few days every month.'

Still a little confused, we asked Scott to elaborate on the problem.

'Each month we get the breakdown of personnel costs for each of the offices from Jeanne in HR. These include things like training and recruiting costs, HR overheads and so on. We also get any changes to the payroll. For some reason, these don't always turn out to be correct. We check them against our numbers but they are usually different, so that's not unusual. But in the past six months many of the office managers have tracked their own expenses. This is both good and bad. It's good because they pick up errors. But usually, most of the errors are in their own spreadsheets so we waste a stack of time tracking down phantom problems.'

'But why doesn't your system match with HR's?'

Scott looked a little uneasy. 'Well, our finance system is in fact linked to the HR payroll system.'

'That's great. But why would there be a difference then?'

'Well, we just don't trust it. So we started asking HR for the reports instead. This started over a year ago now. We think it's better to get the numbers straight from the horse's mouth.'

Scott seemed to run out of time and before we knew it we had left his office. He hadn't really been much help. It seemed that he had completely avoided the issues and pushed the blame on to the HR department. It was time to speak to Jeanne.

Jeanne was also located in Singapore and we found her in her corner office overlooking the bustling city. We explained all that we had seen and heard. She was a good listener, seeming to be interested in what we had to say.

'I knew it. I knew it!' she exclaimed, 'I bet Scott didn't mention that when I asked him to pull the HR numbers from his finance system he declined. He told me that those numbers were just a backup and that the way they had always done business was to get the numbers directly from HR. This is ridiculous. We're not a finance arm. We have our own work to do, like organising and running training, co-ordinating recruitment and ensuring inductees are looked after. On top of all that, we're an advice centre on all HR topics for all the offices in the region.'

After Jeanne had calmed down, we asked her to take us through her issues one by one.

'First of all,' she said, 'the HR and the finance systems are linked but because the data is only uploaded once a week, their information isn't always correct at the end of the month. So instead, they have asked me to give them the reports. I don't have access to the report writer in the HR system, so I have to request reports from the administrator in Sydney. This can take up to a few days so, to save time, I've been doing screen dumps and collating the data into a spreadsheet. This would be bearable if it wasn't for the training information. The HR system doesn't hold any training information so we have to keep track of that ourselves. Usually, the mistake arises because my assistant manually tracks all the training activities for the three hundred employees in the region in another spreadsheet. Then, I combine this with the cost and payroll information in the HR system on my spreadsheet. Between the two of us errors can arise.'

We told Jeanne about the problem the Indonesian manager had picked up when he was allocated a charge for a person that didn't exist in his office.

'Oh yeah,' she sighed, 'that's another problem. These damned systems! Sometimes I think they are far more trouble than they're worth. We have a separate recruiting information system that holds all of the information of potential recruits. If the recruit turns into an employee we have to manually re-key all the data from the recruitment system into the HR system. It's a wicked waste of time and unfortunately in that instance, a candidate who was rejected in the last round of interviews was mistakenly put on the HR system. It can happen pretty easily as I'm sure you can see. It's a mind numbing task.'

We reflected on the situation at hand. The Beast seemed to be running amok. Piles of duplicate information were going in and outdated or no information was coming out. We worked with Jeanne to break down the problem into its components. These were:

- Each office manager and the HR manager were tracking the same training information. This was costing considerable amounts of time and inaccuracy, which in turn resulted in further follow up time with Finance. The main reason the offices tracked the data was because they didn't trust their HR charge allocations.

- Nobody seemed to be able to get timely, accurate information out of the system. This meant that Finance made requests from HR rather than take it directly from their own system. In turn, Jeanne had to build and manage her own spreadsheet of HR information. This too was prone to errors that would impact the accuracy of the HR charge to the offices.

- Personnel information was entered twice into the Beast – once into the recruiting system and then again into the HR system. This was a dull job and prone to errors that could impact on the HR charge allocations to each office.

Jeanne looked over the list as if it smelled. 'The worst part is there's nothing we can do about it.'

We strongly disagreed with this last statement. To us it was obvious that this company's Beast was out of control. Many rules were being violated but the duplication of effort seemed to be the main issue. Yet, the people we'd spoken to seemed resolved to the continuing frustrations and Jeanne had all but given up.

'Why don't you speak to the systems people about it?' we ventured.

If we spoke to IT, what would we ask for?

Jeanne was incredulous. 'Are you kidding? We had no say in purchasing these systems. They're just imposed upon us from up high, very high up. Anyway, even if we did speak to them, what would we ask for?'

Seeing some room to move we said, 'we'd ask them for help around the systems issues you've just described. They're the system experts. Let's go and see them.'

Jeanne looked smug. 'Hope you've got a plane handy. They're all located at Head Office in the States. Nearly all the work on the systems is done from there or in Australia. We could call them.'

After some to-ing and fro-ing we eventually organised a videoconference with some systems people in the States.

At first the systems people were a little difficult. However, when they realised we weren't trying to tell them the system was junk or that they had purchased the wrong ones (after a few off-camera glares at Jeanne whenever her comments strayed that way), things started to progress.

The Beastkeepers were completely amazed that the HR manager didn't have access to the report writer, but even more amazed that, what they called the HR-Finance upload, was causing so many problems. The users were allowed to set any dates they liked for the upload, so the upload time could be set to the last day in each month without any issue whatsoever. This problem was technically solved – all that remained was to smooth the political creases with Scott.

The American systems guys told us they couldn't do anything about the training information. They agreed it should be attached to each person's information in the HR system but that module had not been purchased, so that was that. They suggested we speak to the IT group in Sydney to see if they could make something more robust than a spreadsheet. They agreed to drop them an email to ease the way.

Finally, their eyes lit up when we told them about the double entry with the recruiting database and the HR system. The HR system came with a 'Loader' package that made it possible to load data into the system from several formats. They promised to have a 'play around' with the recruiting package to see if they could export data to a format that the 'Loader' could work with.

After the videoconference Jeanne sat dumbfounded. 'Not in a million years did I think it'd be worthwhile speaking to those guys. They always seem so disinterested in our problems and only interested in their own system ones.'

'Perhaps that's what we're like when we speak to them,' we suggested. 'Anyway, let's follow up those other leads.'

We contacted Sydney about the problem of multiple training spreadsheets. We wanted a single place where both the office managers and HR could view the training information. After two weeks they returned with a simple web based prototype that allowed each office manager to update their own information, and Jeanne could update all of them. So each office continued tracking its own training, removing the need for HR to do this. But HR could still check and confirm it at month end, before passing it to Finance.

Maya was particularly happy about the arrangement because they based the web version on her spreadsheet. She still had the same workload but now she was assured that the figures in the cost report were the same ones she had entered during the month.

The US systems team came back with a straightforward Loader prototype. Recruits' details could be exported from the recruitment system to a spreadsheet file, then the Loader would read the spreadsheet data into the HR system. It saved about 30 percent in time, and removed re-keying errors. It also included a nifty check to ensure that only those recruits with the 'offer accepted' flag could be read into the HR system. No more phantom people!

Scott was less than enthused about using the finance system to access the HR data, although logically he could see that, with the uploads timed to occur at the end each month, there was no reason not to use this data.

Jeanne was thrilled – happy office managers, a happy assistant, and a reduction in her own workload by several days a month. Probably the biggest change was her opinion of the Beastkeepers. She was now their greatest advocate.

INSIGHTS

- The inefficiencies in the Finance and HR departments caused errors that created the need to track information in each local office. The cost of the inefficiencies thus went way beyond those departments.

- The remote location of the IT department immediately created a divide that needed proactively bridging. Although Jeanne knew about problems with the systems, she chose to 'handle them' rather than make an international call. Furthermore, she believed they wouldn't be interested.

Rule Seven Summary

- Don't be put off by setbacks (Mel wasn't!). The business/Beastkeeper divide can be harder to bridge than you would imagine but, when you've done it once, it continues to get easier.

- Inefficiencies can easily be overlooked when the single task appears small. However, if this task is repeated frequently, and in multiple places, then the impact might be huge. Work it out and put a value against it!

- Repeatedly requesting information that everybody knows can, and should, already be available, will definitely lose you customers.

Thinking about your Beast

- Ask your customers (internal and external) if they are doing work to make up for inefficient use of the Beast by your department.

- Write down every instance you can recall when data was re-entered, re-keyed, or re-requested. Estimate how long it takes to do each task and multiply by the number of times this is done each year. How many full time employees does this equate to?

- If you spoke to your Beastkeepers, what would you ask for?

The Eco Plastics Story

'Gus I've got an invoicing problem.' Kate handed him a wad of paperwork. 'They're only part paying. They reckon we over supplied and they sent back the surplus. Do you know anything about it?'

Gus started punching the job number into his computer.

'I've already checked that. The quote matches the amount they say they ordered and they've paid for what they ordered. But the job number shows a much larger quantity was produced.'

'Then what do you need from me?' Gus didn't have time for this.

'Well, what happened to the excess product? Did they return it? And while you're working on that, you might as well find out how the screw up happened.'

Gus had a fair idea how it happened but promised to sort it out. He printed out copies of the original quote and the disputed invoice and compared them to the job bag. Just as he expected, the job bag had initially matched the quote but someone had altered the order.

He put in a call to Jack, who'd made the sale, and left a message. He then set about tracing the missing product by consulting his scheduling history to put a date on the job, that way he would know who was the likely driver.

In the meantime, Jack returned his call. He remembered the job because of the over delivery but vowed that he didn't alter the job bag. No, he didn't know what happened to the excess product but doubted their customer would keep it and claim otherwise.

It took three hours out of Gus's afternoon to work out what had happened.

He had scheduled two orders for the same product to run consecutively. One customer increased their order at the last minute but the wrong job bag was annotated. The extra product was eventually delivered to the right customer but of course the paperwork hadn't caught up.

Gus called Kate to fill her in so she could re-invoice the right customer. Then he called his wife to tell her to expect him home late – about three hours late.

Part Three

Harnessing the Beast

Seeing the potential

If the blind lead the blind, both shall fall into the ditch.

Matthew 15:14

Believe in and apply the Rules

In Part One we introduced the idea of mental constraints that act as blind spots in your thinking, limiting possibilities. Believing in the rules enables you to change your thinking in order that you may see the potential.

Without this fundamental belief, the rules will be applied half-heartedly, if at all, thus diminishing any potential you see. However, with this belief, the rules will be applied zealously and potential will be clearly seen. So, in order to see the potential, you must first believe in the rules.

Once you believe in the rules, then you must apply them. You can approach rule application in two different ways. One is to focus on a particular task, process or problem, and examine it from the perspective of the rules to look for violations. The other is to start with a single rule and seek out business opportunities where that rule is being violated.

This chapter discusses each approach and at the end we revisit Peter, Gus and Kate to see how they began seeing their potential.

Approach One:
Start with a task, process or problem

The diagram below shows you how to employ this approach – look at a single issue (be it a task, process or problem) and then test it against each rule, to find violations.

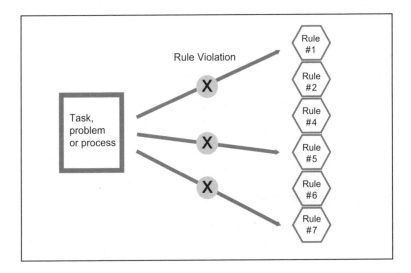

In Part Two we applied a single rule to a task, process or problem. However, the approach taken in the real world was to study the issue and apply each rule to identify which ones were being violated.

For example, the smelter safety case study was described under *Rule Two The Beast is Alive*, because it enabled the people who most needed the information to access it live. It could equally have been included under *Rule Six The Beast Communicates*, because the data wasn't being communicated effectively or easily. (It was extracted from the database, emailed, printed out and then reported orally.)

It is important that you consider all the rules (in all their guises) to identify potential savings and opportunities because you can't know, until you've considered them, which rule violations will yield the greatest prospects.

When using this approach, begin by understanding exactly what the task, process or problem is. For example, when considering a task or process you must understand what it entails. What are the sub-steps? How long does each take? Who is involved and what information is used?

When looking at a problem, ensure you are clear on exactly what the problem is. When did it arise? Where does it occur? In other words, know all the symptoms.

Once you have a thorough understanding of the issue, then you can assess it for rule violations. Go through each rule asking questions to probe for violations. Here are example questions you might ask:

Rule One The Beast is Accessible

- Is all the required information accessible?
- Can everyone who needs it access it?
- Is the information in a usable format?

Rule Two The Beast is Alive

- Does the information arrive at the right time or is there a lag?
- Are decisions delayed?
- Are you or others kept waiting for information?

Rule Three The Beast is Mobile

- Can you use people or information located elsewhere to help solve a problem or improve a process?
- Is this a problem of geography?
- Can you reframe a process to imagine it occurring within the same location?

Rule Four The Beast is Responsive

- Are you getting feedback?
- Is feedback supplied with useful frequency?
- Could feedback have prevented the problem?

Rule Five The Beast is Empowering

- Who is making the decisions – those with the power or those with the appropriate knowledge and skills?
- Can people be empowered with the right information to make the best decisions?
- Could you delegate decision making by improving information access?

Rule Six The Beast Communicates

- Can communication be improved to enhance the task or process, or solve the problem?
- Can the communication medium be changed to save time or to communicate with the right people?

Rule Seven The Beast is Efficient

- Is data being captured more than once?
- Is this costing time and leading to inaccuracies?

Whenever you answer No to a question, you have found a rule violation. Each violation, when corrected, will yield an associated value.

Consider John, the wine shop planner. His task was to create shelf plans with the objective of selling more wine. However, when asked whether he had access to all the information he needed, he answered No. He was drawing these shelf plans blind. He did not know which plans were meeting the objective of selling more wine. Thus, Rule One was being violated and when corrected, provided the feedback to enable John and his team to adapt their task and yield a 3 percent increase in wine sales.

The value of correcting rule violations may also be intangible, for example John and the other shelf planners also improved relations with the wine shop managers. Thus increased job satisfaction can be included as a benefit.

Once all rule violations have been detected, consider the value of correcting each one in order to prioritise action.

Approach Two:
Start with a single Rule

The diagram below shows you how to employ this alternative approach. Look at a single rule and then aim to eliminate any violations wherever they occur to realise hidden opportunities.

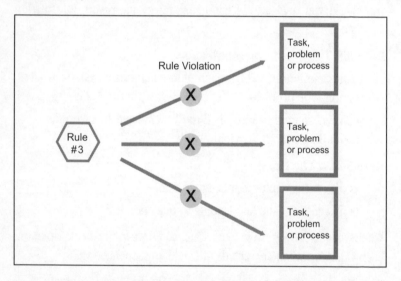

For example, a company may decide that it will benefit most by focusing on a single rule and stamping out violations wherever they are found. It may be a company with a large customer base and multiple interactions, and so it has an increased likelihood of violating *Rule Seven The Beast is Efficient*. Therefore, by focusing on just this rule, the company will make big wins.

Alternatively, the company decides to harness its Beast by encouraging its workforce to become digital thinkers. The company believes the best way to foster this change is by championing one rule at a time.

Being a customer focused company, *Rule Four The Beast is Responsive* is selected to start the change process.

The point of starting with a single rule is to use the Beast to realise hidden opportunities. Eventually, all rules will be addressed to maximise the company's potential. As you will see in the next instalment of the Eco Plastics Story, this approach doesn't necessarily take a protracted route. A rule violation assessment was performed at Eco Plastics by applying each rule in turn to calculate the location of the biggest prize and then prioritise action.

Believe in and apply the Rules

- Choose a rule application approach
- List rule violations
- Value benefits to prioritise action

The Eco Plastics Story

By the time Eco Plastics sought outside help, the company was accelerating inexorably downhill. The management team had argued themselves into a state of paralysis.

We spent the first morning listening to Peter, Gus and Kate explaining the business's problems from each of their perspectives. They all had ideas about how to proceed and all had reasons why everyone else's ideas lacked merit.

Peter had grown the business through high volume, low margin sales. He believed that since the factory was paid for, any sales are good sales, and that while demand exceeded supply, they should just pump up the volume at any price. In the past, they had borrowed money to invest in new equipment to support this strategy and it worked through the bounty years, earning Eco Plastics handsome returns. However, more recently, Eco Plastics had been forced to consolidate their factories back to one site yet Peter still believed the answer to their dilemma lay in pumping up the volume.

Kate remained adamant that this strategy was driving them into the ground, as more and more low margin work, with shrinking volumes, resulted in ever decreasing profits. Kate's concern focused on production costs, in particular waste and labour. She floated the idea of reducing the operation to a four day week but they all worried that, if the operation continued shrinking, it would ultimately vanish.

Gus shared Kate's concern about production costs but his focus was on the main overhead of electricity – a cost that had recently and unexpectedly gone up by 15 percent due to an unexplained increase in usage. But his plan for purchasing monitoring equipment to work out where the increased power was being consumed had been vetoed by the others. He was also looking into diversifying their product output by finding a market for an extruded waste product.

Of course, it didn't come out wrapped in so much clarity, but rather all in an acrimonious tumble of claim and counter-claim. Still, it was an important exercise for allowing the managers to unload and getting them to agree that they were stuck. The exercise also identified the business problems facing Eco Plastics and enabled the assembled group to summarise the issues. The issues separated neatly into external and internal categories.

The external issues included the rising price of scrap and the declining sell price, which combined to reduce profit margins. Also, they needed to ascertain whether finding a market for Gus's waste by-product was viable. Internal issues involved an unexplained hike in the cost of electricity and options regarding reduced labour hours and waste reduction.

The team spent the morning arguing in circles, however they

ultimately agreed on this external/internal division of issues, and on the following points:

- They could not agree a way forward.
- They were not working together to solve the company's problems.
- They had no clear plan for assessing which of the many options would have the greatest positive business impact.
- They did not know by how much they could reduce their prices and remain profitable.
- They were unsure whether some sales were in fact loss makers.
- They were unsure how much more product they could produce.

When this list was written down for all to see, it became obvious that half of these items involved information deficits. Also obvious, was that provision of this information would enable the other half to be addressed. Once they possessed the necessary information, they would be working together from a collectively informed position.

Applying the Rules

Given that information deficits were contributing significantly to the Eco Plastics' difficulties, we explained the concept of the Beast and the rules for harnessing the Beast.

We asked Peter, Gus and Kate to work through each of the rules and assess whether or not Eco Plastics was violating any of them. Peter was initially concerned that we were *pushing our own barrow* and wasting their time. We explained that because they had been going over the problems relentlessly (and fruitlessly) for months, a fresh approach was needed to yield fresh thinking.

Our role was to guide their thinking with selected questions but to ultimately allow them to solve their own problems. This would allow them to take ownership of any solutions. Ownership would then ensure that solutions, once identified, would be implemented and sustained. Also, allowing Peter, Gus and Kate to solve their own problems would enable them to reclaim their lost confidence.

We went through the rules one at a time.

Rule One The Beast is Accessible

We asked them whether information was available to everyone who needs it, in an accessible format.

'Absolutely,' said Kate, who routinely generated profit and loss reports for the company and one-off reports as requested by Peter and Gus.

Gus gently countered Kate's emphatic response. 'Well that can't be the case if we can't agree on solutions because we're missing information.'

'And if we're talking about accessible format,' Peter hesitated to find the right words, 'put it this way, I have to be in the right mood to face one of your reports.'

Kate was genuinely surprised by Gus and Peter's responses and was eager to fill the gaps, in content and style, so that she could again have confidence in her reports.

We interjected to ask what information they needed to help move them forward and instructed them not to be constrained by the information they *thought* was available.

They agreed to focus on the external issues first and developed a wish list of information they would ideally like to have. They quickly agreed that what they wanted was a breakdown of profit by product. In order to know what the profit is on each product, they needed three pieces of information:

1 The product recipe

Eco Plastics produced five core products, each with possible variations, resulting in almost thirty different products.

2 The prices for different types of scrap

Great variability existed in both the supply and quality of scrap. Consequently scrap prices fluctuated daily.

3 Sales price for each product

Regardless of what the prevailing scrap price may be, the sale price is capped by the cost of virgin product. If Eco Plastics' customers can source non-recycled materials for X amount, then recycled plastics must be priced less than X, to remain viable.

For the internal issues they needed to know what the wastage was, expressed as a pound value. They had previously dealt with the electricity costs and marked it as a lesser priority because it was likely to yield only a relatively small win. Similarly, although Gus's idea for a waste by-product had merit, as long as the managers lacked information around the profitability of their existing products they had no way of judging whether his idea was worth pursuing.

Consequently, they agreed that the first thing to do was address this fundamental lack of information around product profitability. Kate, as the company's information gatekeeper (its Beastkeeper), knew that this information was available. It is just that typically, the information she provided was confined to average price per unit and average cost per unit. Her reports didn't address the specifics of product profitability.

Once they had ascertained that the required information existed, they moved the discussion on to the second part of the rule and considered what each of them wanted in terms of an accessible format.

Kate typically produced numerical reports, free of graphics, unaware of how inaccessible Peter and Gus found this style of information presentation. And because she didn't understand their information needs, she hadn't realised how simple it was to address them.

She was very comfortable with numbers but Peter's eyes glazed over whenever one of Kate's information reports was wafted before him. Kate loved numbers. Peter hated them.

Further discussion revealed that Kate used information to explain anomalies and answer Peter and Gus's questions, rather than as a holistic system capable of guiding crucial company decisions.

Kate's Beast was definitely unharnessed.

Rule Two The Beast is Alive

We explained this rule and asked whether information was available live. They couldn't immediately see how this rule could be put into practice at Eco Plastics because they were initially constrained by what they thought was possible and what they believed to be the limits of their Beast. After encouragement, they dared to think about what was ideal.

'The sales guys could benefit from live information on scrap prices,' Gus ventured. 'Is that what you mean?'

'We could all benefit from live scrap prices,' confirmed Peter.

'And if they could schedule their jobs live, that'd stop us double-booking jobs,' Gus continued.

'You know, if they could schedule the jobs live they could factor in economies of scale and pass the savings onto the customer.'

One idea prompted another and Kate jotted them all down.

Rule Three The Beast is Mobile

At first, Peter struggled to see the difference between this rule and Rule Two because ideas about the sales team accessing live scrap prices and entering jobs into the schedule meant being mobile.

We pointed out the more subtle changes of enabling the sales team to access the schedule remotely, changes that would create boundary-less behaviour. No longer would sales and production be disconnected and it is possible that other benefits would flow in the future as a result of this increased agility.

Rule Four The Beast is Responsive

We challenged the team on whether feedback and organisational response are instantaneous.

Kate considered this for a moment. 'Whenever we have an invoicing problem it takes ages to sort it out. Is that the sort of thing you mean?'

'I think it means like when sales increase suddenly but scrap buying doesn't respond quickly enough,' Gus said. 'Is that right?'

'It could be anything that costs you because of a delayed response,' we said.

'It costs us when money is outstanding,' said Kate.

'And it definitely costs us when we incur downtime because we run out of scrap. Gives me a headache too,' Gus added.

Rule Five The Beast is Empowering

We already knew that the Eco Plastics management team was struggling to make decisions. When we explained the rule, along with the importance of assessing the size of the prize, the certainty of success and the cost of failing, Peter, Gus and Kate were all nodding their agreement.

We spent additional time on this rule underlining the importance of valuing potential action. Kate had already done this when she calculated the potential savings in electricity. She was right in suggesting they initially direct their energies elsewhere.

Rule Six The Beast Communicates

The management team was adamant that they already communicated effectively. Again, they were constrained by their thinking about what effective communication meant. Eventually we reminded them of something Gus had revealed earlier – that the scheduling sometimes gets double-booked.

'I get it,' said Peter, 'if we were communicating effectively, that wouldn't happen.'

'Same for errors on the job sheets,' added Gus, 'what generally happens is that any changes will get phoned in and whoever answers the phone will alter the job sheet.'

'Not always accurately,' Kate confirmed, winking at Gus.

Rule Seven The Beast is Efficient

When they heard the title of this rule Peter, Gus and Kate roared with laughter, all agreeing that if they'd learned one thing today, it was that their Beast was definitely not efficient.

We explained that the rule meant that data is captured and stored once.

Straight away Kate pointed out a violation. 'The job sheet errors. Details of the quotes get put into the system but the job sheets are manually written. Then invoices are raised from the job sheets.'

'Why do we do it that way?' Peter wanted to know.

Kate shrugged. 'It just developed that way because there are two different systems. Do you think it's possible to connect them? It'd be brilliant if we can.'

When the management team finished considering all the rules, they had a list of information they needed to access, thoughts about how they'd like that information presented, and a host of other ideas for harnessing their Beast.

Additionally, the exercise had shifted their attitude from one of scepticism to one of whole-hearted belief in the rules.

Tackling the divide

I've always understood the raw power of technology but until I understood the business perspective, I never realised its value.

Nick Kent
Global IT Project Manager, Shell

No matter which approach you choose to apply the rules, applying them is all about seeing the potential. Once you can see the potential then you can realise it.

The biggest blocker to realising the potential is the business/ Beastkeeper divide we identified in Part One. Recall that this is a functional divide with the Beastkeepers on one side and business people on the other side, each doing their own thing. The result is that the Beastkeepers' objectives and our business objectives often operate in parallel. This situation is perpetuated by our failure to understand the Beast's capabilities and the Beastkeepers' failure to understand our business needs.

It is important at this point to also revisit the concept of Beastkeepers. We identified them as either those buzzing away in the information technology department, or as information gatekeepers (knowledge managers, accountants, or anyone involved in producing reports). Although we collectively labelled them the Beastkeepers, there is a distinction to be made based on whether they manage the Beast or the Beast's data: technical Beastkeepers or information Beastkeepers.

The terminology we use serves a purpose – it helps clarify complex issues. Just as the Beast metaphor gives form to the amorphous nature of business technology, so the concept of a business/Beastkeeper divide seeks to contain a nebulous range of relationships.

For example, in one case study the divide existed between Jane, the data processing clerk, and her department's 'systems guy'. In another, the divide was effectively between the marketing department, where John drew his wine shop shelf plans, and the warehouse. However, for Jeanne, the Singapore based HR Manager, the divide was split between her and the company's systems people, spread from the United States to Australia.

Notice how each of the Beastkeepers' roles is different. Jane's is a single technical Beastkeeper allocated to her department. John's was an information Beastkeeper located in another business department and Jeanne's were a collection of technical Beastkeepers spread across two continents.

The major symptomatic factors for these divides were also different. For Jane the divide manifested through anonymity (she didn't even know his name), for John it was department boundaries, and in Jeanne's case, mutual hostility and physical distance.

The balance of Part Three explores this divide. First by helping you to recognise and understand divide symptoms and then by discussing a process for bridging the divide. We also revisit the Eco Plastics story to see how Peter, Gus and Kate realised Eco Plastics' potential.

Finally, we pull it all together in a step-by-step summary to make it easy for you to take action.

Recognising the divide

The first step in tackling the divide is to recognise it. Recognising the divide between you and your Beastkeepers is not as difficult as it may appear.

Consider three key symptoms:

1 Business is blind to its Beast.

2 Business underestimates its Beast.

3 Business assumes Beastkeepers are mind readers.

1 Business is blind to its Beast

In most of the case studies in Part Two, the overwhelming telltale sign of a divide was that the business people did not consider using the Beast to solve their problem.

Recall the mental model described in Part One. People have boundaries that constrain their thinking about what is possible. If the Beast isn't even considered as a possible answer then an entire avenue of solutions will be completely beyond their reach.

Think back to William and his time management problem, a result of inefficient communication. The combined effects of cutbacks and a push to encourage peer networking overwhelmed William, yet it hadn't occurred to him that the Beast could solve what had become his biggest problem. Nor did it occur to any of his peers, who were no doubt also experiencing the same problem. And why not? Because the Beast did not show up on their mental radars, they could not see beyond their mental barriers.

If you review the case studies the same symptom is visible in most of them. The Beast was not seen as a potential tool to be utilised in solving the business issue at hand. In the same way that if a carpenter doesn't have a screwdriver, none of his solutions will involve screws, so it is that without the Beast, none of the business solutions will involve the massive technology resource currently available.

The result of this thinking is wasted resources and limited solutions. It can impact every part of your business from sales to production, from customer service to human resources. The companies that exploit this new lever first will dominate their industries, while their competitors, having paid for the Beast, continue addressing business issues with one powerful arm tied behind their backs.

2 Business underestimates its Beast

The second symptom of the divide occurs when business people consider the Beast when tackling business problems but assume their limited understanding represents the full potential. In this instance, it's not that the business person doesn't consider using the Beast, it's just that the use is limited by what they know, rather than what is possible.

Consider Mike, who was trying to pack more sweets in Rule Three. He realised that sharing information from other sites around the world could be helpful for increasing machine speeds and reducing costs. However, he limited his use of the Beast to making telephone calls and then despaired of ever collating all the required information.

Only when he met Sonia, the technical Beastkeeper, did a feasible solution became clear. More than simply responding to Mike's business problem, the intranet proved an excellent way of enabling sites the world over to drive a range of production improvements.

Mike acknowledged he would never have thought of this solution and confessed that it was even more unlikely that he would have involved the information technology department. He just couldn't see what they had to do with production problems.

Understanding the Beast's capabilities isn't confined to appreciating the power of a system. Typically, business people overestimate the time and cost of implementing a Beast solution and this is another aspect of not understanding the Beast's capability. Recall Steve's response to the suggestion of using the intranet for posting safety information at the smelter: *I don't think it'll be easy. The systems people are always flat out.*

It's true that not long ago it may have taken a room full of programmers to get information to you in a particular format from the other side of the company, or even the other side of the wall. These days, many powerful programs allow information to be taken and manipulated across many disparate systems and displayed in various formats, such as spreadsheet files, web pages, documents and emails. By overestimating the difficulty of the task, business people discard excellent opportunities for improvement.

The key point is that without an understanding of the Beast's capability, many effective solutions are overlooked. The divide exists in your organisation if business people are not involving their Beastkeepers when pondering a problem or contemplating a solution.

3 Business assumes Beastkeepers are mind readers

Most business managers are clear on their goals and the major issues in their department but they rarely write them down to share with their own direct reports. It isn't surprising then that their Beastkeepers do not fully understand the business goals and issues. This is another indicator of the presence of a divide. The business knows what it wants but not necessarily how to get it, whereas the Beastkeepers could supply it, if only they knew what was wanted.

The underlying assumption from business is that the Beastkeepers do in fact understand the business issues sufficiently and therefore will point out opportunities if they exist.

Consider again Jane, the data processing clerk. Jane understood that one of her primary goals was the reduction in account processing time. She also knew that she wasted time because of the way the batch processing worked. What she didn't know was how to correct it. On the other hand, her systems guy (his name was Kevin by the way) knew nothing of Jane's batch size issue. He had no real understanding of the business problem. But when asked for a particular change to be made, he did it within moments.

Similarly, Daniel and Charles, the management consultants, were struggling with inadequate information when all the time their accounting and marketing people (their Beastkeepers) held what they needed. Daniel and Charles didn't know it existed, so didn't ask for it. The Beastkeepers didn't know how valuable it was to the business, so didn't offer it.

This is the strange juxtaposition that accompanies the divide. Side by side are people with questions and people with answers but neither group seems aware of the other sufficiently to reach out and make the necessary contact.

Understanding the divide

In order to work out the best way to tackle the divide, we must understand how it arose and why it is sustained.

The divide is a product of the rapid evolution of the Beast and the delay in business people changing their thinking about what is now possible. There is no single cause and no single group of people to blame for the divide. Rather, it is a combination of factors that contribute to the growth of any divide. Therefore, by understanding the nature of these factors, they can be better overcome.

Below are some of the factors that we have seen contributing to the divide. However, since every individual and every organisation is different, not all of our factors will be evident within your divide and you will see others not listed here. The important point is to develop an understanding of how the divide has arisen and is sustained in your organisation, because such an understanding will increase your effectiveness in bridging it.

Factors contributing to the divide include:

1 Too busy servicing
2 New is better
3 No natural relationship
4 Company culture
5 Poor communication

Factor 1   Too busy servicing

As with most people in today's business world, Beastkeepers are very busy. However, it is what they are busy doing that is critical.

Collectively they have a broad range of work requirements, often dividing their time between activities such as:

- Maintaining, repairing and securing systems

- Extracting data and compiling reports
- Assessing the purchase of new systems
- Upgrading to the latest versions of software
- Adding new user accounts

When you consider the tasks listed above, the majority are necessary for the successful functioning of the business but are unlikely to transform the business. Just keeping the Beast well fed and groomed is a massive operation, one that regularly consumes most, if not all, of the Beastkeepers' time. But most of these activities are well-defined services requiring little or no consultation with the business. This often leads to a perception by the business of a specialist service only to be called upon when needed, just as you would call on a plumber to fix a leaking pipe.

In this type of relationship, it's unlikely that business people will approach Beastkeepers to discuss anything other than technical problems – certainly not business problems. That would be equivalent to approaching your plumber with family issues.

Factor 2   New is better

You may be thinking that you don't have a divide because your Company Information Officer (CIO) is focused on extracting maximum value from technology. Nowadays this is often a stated company goal. However, how does this ideal manifest itself? Typically, we find a strategic CIO focused on the search for large, new technology levers to propel the company ahead of the competition. These are often exciting projects promising even more exciting results but the experiences of the last few years demonstrate that the end result is a massive amount of effort focused on the implementation of the new system which everyone assumes will fix all problems. Unfortunately it doesn't but by then it's too late; people have been distracted from making the most of what already exists by focusing on the new arrival.

There is another driver feeding the belief that new is better, one that is all to do with people and their natural desires.

In general, technical people get great personal satisfaction from striving to understand and master a subject. Once their job is mastered, a technical person seeks to continue expanding their knowledge. For a technical Beastkeeper this often means learning new technologies or new ways of doing things. Therefore, they are personally interested in new technologies, new systems and new programs rather than existing capabilities. Suddenly you see why jobs related to new technologies are so popular – for a technical person it's like being paid to play with the latest toys!

Factor 3   No natural relationship

Other than to get a problem fixed or a report produced, are there any regular reasons why you would meet with Beastkeepers? Typically not, and this means that there are few opportunities for a relationship to develop between business and Beastkeepers.

Beastkeepers are often located in different departments or locations to gain benefits of centralisation. This has multiple consequences. By being housed remotely from the business, there is little chance for informal contact and social relationships to develop. At best, communication will happen over the phone or via email and will be initiated for some work-based reason, often a problem or frustration. This perpetuates the 'us and them' mentality on both sides of the divide and removes the natural networking opportunities that work so well in other areas of business.

Many companies have taken this distinction between business and Beastkeepers one step further and outsourced the whole Beastkeeping function, no longer seeing it as core to the business process. This strongly reflects the service-based relationship existing between Beastkeepers and the rest of the organisation, making formal the distinction of 'us and them'.

Factor 4   Company culture

Does your company culture promote building relationships between business and Beastkeepers or does it do the opposite? Are you encouraged to approach Beastkeepers for help or are you charged for it? When 'quality' became the buzzword in industry, members of the QA Departments were automatically involved with all aspects of the business. If a piece of equipment changed or a new raw material sourced, QA had to be advised and included. Rarely is there the same inclusive force for maximising business/Beastkeeper dialogue. Other than where the business has specific questions to be answered regarding technology or information, Beastkeepers are rarely invited to get involved with business activities.

With the mounting disappointment at return on investment for technology, the pressure is now on for IT departments to function as proper businesses. The natural response of these departments is to pull the lever they have control over. Thus they reduce costs by reducing PCs, minimising support, implementing new systems to reduce future maintenance, and so on.

Although these activities are valuable from a straight cost saving angle, they do not promote the benefit that can be gained from making further use of existing technology. This is a classic instance of sub-optimising the whole to optimise the part. The impact on the divide is to focus efforts on reducing costs in the information technology department rather than increasing benefit in the business.

Factor 5   Poor communications

There has long been frustration on both sides of the divide. Business people are frustrated that their requests are not implemented quickly, that many of their requests are rejected, and that often the outcomes are not what they expected. They also get frustrated with the seeming need to understand a huge amount of technical jargon in order to communicate their needs.

On the other side, the Beastkeepers are often extremely frustrated at the lack of priority on incoming work as well as the nebulous and changing nature of specifications. There's nothing more frustrating for system builders if the specifications change halfway through the project. The result can often force the project team to start again from scratch. Business people seem to have limited understanding that by changing the specification the entire system may have to be redesigned. Thus requests from the business take longer to implement, cost more than anticipated, and don't materialise as expected... and the divide widens.

The whole communication issue then gets more complicated again when you consider the number of different people on the business side who can make requests, coupled with the large number of specialised Beastkeepers – all looking after their own particular part of the Beast. If uncontrolled on both sides of the divide, there is massive scope for duplication of work, lack of resource prioritisation and misunderstanding as to the business benefit.

These five factors represent those we have seen most frequently in companies. No doubt you can also recognise them in the earlier case studies. For instance, Jane's Beastkeeper was pre-occupied servicing the company's Beast, whereas for John, no natural relationship existed between him and his information Beastkeeper in the warehouse. Poor Jeanne though was experiencing a major divide with at least three significant factors: no natural relationship, company culture, and poor communication.

Your own situation will be unique, with a mixture of factors each carrying its own importance. The critical point is that you start to understand your factors in order to help you move ahead and bridge the divide.

Bridging the divide

At this point in the book you:

- believe in the rules and can apply them to see the hidden potential in your business, and

- recognise and understand the business/Beastkeeper divide as the main reason this potential has not yet been realised.

Having gained an understanding of what the divide looks like and why it exists, you are perfectly positioned to decide how to bridge it.

The exact tasks you have to perform will depend on the type of opportunity as well as the organisational resources available to you. However, there are three generic steps to undertake *before* you jump into action.

Assuming that you have applied the rules to identify an opportunity, you must now:

1 Explain the potential

2 Articulate the divide

3 Strategise and plan

Many people get so excited on seeing an opportunity for the first time that they are tempted to skip these three steps and spring straight into action. If you do decide to skip these critical steps then be prepared to fail.

In the case studies, to maintain clarity, we did not highlight these preparatory steps when we applied the rules. It was our role as consultants to ensure the divide was bridged smoothly. For example, when William was overloaded and needed to free up his time by getting the Beast to help him communicate, we went to talk to Seamus the system Beastkeeper.

By revisiting this case study, we can discuss what we did in terms of the three steps outlined above. Firstly, we forced ourselves to **explain the potential** improvements for William. These included:

- why his situation had suddenly worsened (cutbacks combined with a push to network with peers)

- the potential benefits (saving at least one day per week as well as more accurate information transfer)

- what we could envisage as an end result (implementation of a communication strategy combining web, email, phone and face-to-face interaction).

Secondly, we asked William to arrange for us to meet Seamus, at a time convenient for Seamus. This meeting was not about taking action, it was all about **articulating the divide**. We didn't just turn up to Seamus's office unannounced and ask him to implement a change for us. We explained the potential and explored what factors would need to be addressed. As it turned out, the main cause of the divide was that Seamus knew nothing of William's problems. So our challenge was to bring them together to discuss the issue.

Thirdly, we arranged for William and Seamus to meet, specifically to agree what needed to be done and therefore address the main cause of this divide. Note that we did not agree a solution with Seamus. Doing so would undoubtedly have caused problems later, because we did not know all the details of William's communication needs. It was essential that Seamus and William discussed the problem and agreed the specification thus bridging their divide. Their meeting was all about the **strategy and planning** of what needed to be done. Even by the end of this meeting no change had actually occurred.

We now consider each of these three steps in greater detail so you can better understand their importance.

1   Explain the potential

A big difference exists between seeing potential for yourself and being able to express it well enough for others to both see it, and be motivated to take action. Often it is not until you try to express something in words that you see the holes in your argument or realise that a critical piece of need-building evidence is missing.

For example, if you were responsible for the financial systems in a business, and I told you that my biggest problem was not receiving estimates prior to work being done by contractors, what would your reaction be? You would likely empathise but not be moved to take action. After all, getting estimates is not your job. However, if I showed you the real data for last month showing we'd spent £5.5 million, almost three times more than the estimates of £1.8 million, you might take me more seriously. You'd probably immediately initiate a rule in your department to ensure no invoice was paid that exceeded the estimate. After all, your system does hold all the estimate data, it is just that your team don't usually use it.

This example may seem trivial and obvious but it is a real example from one of the world's leading companies. In fact, they had talked about the need to improve estimating for years without taking action. Why? Because, until the issue was properly explained and the evidence valued, nobody took it seriously.

A critical aspect of this explanation is to value the benefit. Without a clear benefit, the chances of change happening are very slim. Being clear about the benefit will not only help you enrol others but also help you maintain your own conviction in the face of the inevitable barriers.

Remember that there are many different types of benefit such as:

- saving time
- saving costs
- boosting morale
- working safer
- increasing profit
- responding to customers faster
- increasing market share.

This is by no means an exhaustive list and, depending on your situation, some will be viewed as more valuable than others. The key is to identify the important benefits and estimate a value for each.

Let's suppose you identify an opportunity to feed information from your call centre to your team in the research and development department. You decide it would be beneficial to see a daily update of all the problems, flagged for each product. In addition, you want this information converted to pounds. This information will empower you to make better business decisions and enable your team to respond immediately to feedback.

You sit down with Beverly, Beastkeeper for the call centre system, and explain what you want to do. She tells you it's impossible because you need information from the finance system and the call centre system and they are not linked.

At this point you might throw your hands up and walk out disappointed. But stop for one moment and think about what Beverly has told you. She has stated that the two systems are not linked and therefore the information you require cannot be accessed in a single move. Yet you know that if you wanted each dataset separately, that it is technically possible.

Can the data be extracted separately and combined in some way? Why should this be too difficult? Well, of course, it is not too difficult if you know that the result of having this information is worth £300,000 a year. Why will this information save so much money? Because research and development will be able to work on the problems costing the company the most money rather than those with the highest frequency of occurrence.

Beverly was really telling you that she couldn't immediately see how to do it and, as there was no apparent benefit, she had better things to do than find a way to make it happen.

Explain the potential

- Clearly describe the potential
- Spell out and value the benefits
- Use evidence to motivate action

---

2 Articulate the divide

Even when you have clearly explained the potential you've seen, there is much to be done before it can be realised. The next step is to articulate the divide by assessing what factors are in play.

Undoubtedly, there will be many factors contributing to the divide in your company but you don't need to correct them all before realising benefits. However, it is critical to identify the factors that are preventing the specific potential you've seen from being realised.

Use the factors described in *Understanding the divide* as a first step to helping you see those affecting your situation. Remember, these are a starting point and you should identify your factors as specifically as possible. This may mean adding your own factors to the list.

Reconsider the example where you asked Beverly for information from both the call centre and finance systems in order to prioritise work in research and development. A certain factor to explore in this case would be *Factor 5 Poor communication* as multiple people must interact. You know that information must be gathered from two systems so at least two Beastkeepers would need to be involved before a solution could be determined. It would be impossible for Beverly on her own to make it happen, as she is not responsible for the finance system. Possibly there are even more and you must try to identify them.

Once Beverly understands just how beneficial it would be to make this happen, she can then help identify the major factors causing this divide. For example, Beverly might see the major difficulty as limited resources for working out how to combine information from each system, a clear case of *Factor 1 Too busy servicing*. Alternatively, she may tell you that finance are very protective of their information and have a blanket policy of not allowing any data to leave their department, except in their official end-of-month reports. You may decide this situation is not directly covered by the list of five factors we gave you so you should create your own: *Factor 6 Departmental Policy*.

The approach required to bridge the divide for each of these two simple responses from Beverly are quite different, so it is vital you find out which is in play to know the best approach.

When you have made a list of the factors affecting your divide, prioritise them in terms of the influence you believe they have and, therefore, the attention you need to pay to each. You will then have a clear picture of your divide and be ready to work out how best to bridge it.

Articulate the divide

● Review the list of factors provided

● Identify the factors of your divide

● Articulate and rank these factors

3 Strategise and plan

Once you have explained the potential you see and articulated your divide, you must then calculate the best way to tackle it. This means devising a **strategy** and, typically, this comes down to common sense and people skills.

In Beverly's example, let's consider the strategy if limited resource really is the major factor. Here it is critical to determine who is in a position to provide the necessary resource. This may be a case of convincing Beverly's supervisor to rearrange the internal resource or it may be a situation where the best approach is to get external help through your own department. Therefore, your strategy will be directed at either Beverly's manager or your own. Using the evidence and benefits already determined will make this decision easy.

However, if the second scenario is correct and the major factor to overcome is the finance department's data protectiveness, then your strategy would be different. In this situation you will need to approach a senior member of the finance team to get agreement. You may even need to enrol assistance from your own manager to do this or even go higher up the hierarchy. Identifying factors to overcome is not enough in and of itself. You need to devise a strategy.

Once the factors are clear, identifying the best strategy is usually not a difficult step as it will be clear what needs to be done. The skill is in creating the right interactions in the right order to efficiently realise the opportunity.

It is also critical at this point to **plan** exactly what needs to be done. It is amazing how many times great opportunities are not realised because, whilst everyone appears to be in agreement, the exact steps have not been determined.

A major aid in overcoming this problem is to always develop a detailed specification of what is required. The business or the Beastkeeper in isolation cannot do this. They must plan it together. In fact, the best approach we have seen is to produce a mock up, or prototype, of the end result so that everyone is clear what they are working towards.

This may seem over the top but, as soon as you start to discuss it, you will quickly find out one of two things. Either:

- everybody has the same picture, or
- people have very different pictures.

In the first case it will only take a few minutes to confirm your agreement. In the second case a few extra minutes at this point will save hours of costly rework later.

A common example is when someone requests a report from the Beastkeeper. They might ask for a report on 'last month's sales'. In their mind, the requester imagines a report that shows sales by product for each week of last month. However, the Beastkeeper interprets this as a report showing the total monthly sales by geographical region. Both are reports of 'last month's sales' but the end result will be delays, rework and frustration (and a wider divide!). Avoid these situations by sitting down and agreeing exactly what is expected before work begins.

Strategise and plan

- Start with the ranked factors
- Construct a strategy to overcome these
- Agree a plan (including a mock-up)

The Eco Plastics Story

We introduced the concepts of Beastkeepers and the business/Beastkeeper divide. We identified Kate as the information Beastkeeper since, as the accountant, she produced all reports. Eco Plastics also had a technical Beastkeeper. This was a contractor they used for installing the components of their Beast but other than that, they only called him out when something failed.

When it became apparent that the technical Beastkeeper would be required, Kate expressed concern about the cost. She was adamant that they couldn't afford to buy any new bits of kit or pay for too much faffing about with the existing systems.

We reassured her that the process was all about finding ways of using their existing infrastructure better. Also, that the information garnered from considering the rules, would form the basis of a brief for their technical Beastkeeper. Once he understood their information needs and business problems, he would be well placed to advise what could be achieved both quickly and inexpensively.

Clearly, a number of factors were contributing to the business/Beastkeeper divide:

- The technical Beastkeeper serviced the Beast rather than consulted the business.
- No natural relationship existed and few reasons for contact existed between the outsourced Beastkeeper and the business.
- The company culture saw consulting with the external Beastkeeper as an expense rather than an opportunity.

The act of listing these factors exposed Eco Plastics' relationship with its technical Beastkeeper and helped them to understand their business/Beastkeeper divide.

However, this did little to allay Kate's concerns about costs which we identified as the major factor for the management team to overcome. After all, it was our job in this instance to bridge the divide on their behalf.

So we encouraged them to use the results of their rule violation assessment to clearly describe the potential benefits they had identified. Compelling them to write out and value each benefit was sufficient to motivate them to take action.

It also enabled them to prioritise the list so that when they sat down with Sanjay, their technical Beastkeeper, they knew that the top priority was to be able to know the profitability of any given product at any given time. This information would satisfy their most pressing information deficits and guide crucial decision making about how to stop the business from haemorrhaging.

Ready, steady, GO!

The definition of insanity: continually performing the same actions yet expecting different results.

Proverb

Take action!

Up until now we have talked about seeing the potential and preparing to realise it. We have deliberately separated this action-oriented section to highlight the distinction between planning and doing. Often, in spite of having done all the thinking about what to do, initiatives fail to make the hurdle from planning to action. Too many times the action step is assumed... but never done!

To ensure the opportunity you see is truly realised three key things must now happen:

- Decide to do it
- Do it
- Measure the impact

All change takes effort, usually from more than one person. Couple this with the fact that most people are busy and all too easily the actions required to drive home the change get forgotten in the here and now activity of every day life. It requires a definite, conscious decision that this is going to happen, that you are not going to let it slip off the agenda. You must *decide to do it*.

Do not leave it to chance. Do not assume that because the potential has been seen, the divide has been recognised and understood with bridging plans put in place, that the potential will automatically be realised. You must make sure that you, or whoever needs to, take the actions necessary to realise the benefits. Make sure you *do it*.

It is a fact that result-led change is much more successful than purely process led change. When people see the true impact of their actions they get excited. They are more likely to support further change and suggest more opportunities. In large companies today, many people are effectively working in the dark; carrying out their assigned tasks without ever really seeing the result of their labour. If you want to ensure your change is sustained then show people what happened: *measure the impact*.

The *Take action!* step completes our process for setting about harnessing your Beast.

You've seen that thinking, specifically digital thinking, is the new big lever in your organisation. You can apply the Rules and uncover hidden potential. You appreciate that the biggest barrier to realising this potential is the business/Beastkeeper divide, yet remain confident of bridging it. In other words, you are ready.

Opposite is a summary of Part Three captured in a BEAST! mnemonic to help you remember the key steps:

> **B**elieve in, and apply the Rules
>
> **E**xplain the potential
>
> **A**rticulate the divide
>
> **S**trategise and plan
>
> **T**ake action!

To further help you get started, we have included a Digital Health Check as an appendix. It is a questionnaire that only takes fifteen minutes to complete and provides an indication of the opportunity that exists in your organisation, as well as an idea of the size of your divide. Alternatively, you can visit www.harnessthebeast.com, complete the questionnaire online and get the Beast to tally the scores.

Whatever your next step, have a go and remember in the world of the Beast, there is such a thing as improvement for free!

Believe in and apply the Rules

- Choose a rule application approach
- List rule violations
- Value benefits to prioritise action

Explain the potential

- Clearly describe the potential
- Spell out and value the benefits
- Use evidence to motivate action

Articulate the divide

- Review the list of factors provided
- Identify the factors of your divide
- Articulate and rank these factors

Strategise and plan

- Start with the ranked factors
- Construct a strategy to overcome these
- Agree a plan (including a mock-up)

Take action!

- Decide to do it
- Do it
- Measure the impact

The Eco Plastics Story

When Peter, Gus and Kate finally sat down with Sanjay to agree a strategy and plan, they also discussed their most highly ranked divide factor – that of cost. This frank discussion enabled Sanjay to better appreciate Eco Plastics' precarious financial situation so that he could consult to the business rather than merely service its Beast.

Sanjay's solution was ingenious. Using the company's existing database and existing information, he used a basic spreadsheet package to develop a simple tool for determining the profitability of each product. He effectively trained their Beast to tell them when a product would be profitable, marginal, or unprofitable, using a standard traffic light code:

- **Green** meant that the product would generate enough profit to cover both fixed and variable costs.
- **Amber** meant that the product would generate enough profit to cover variable costs.
- **Red** meant that the product would generate a loss and should not be run.

Peter was excited because the traffic light code was easy to understand and it meant that he could pump up the volume and produce even more amber products.

Gus was concerned because they still needed to know the right mix of green and amber products to ensure their fixed costs were covered.

However, Kate knew that she could produce a monthly report tracking the ratio of green and amber products to ensure sales were targeted profitably. Now she knew how to produce these reports graphically so they would carry more meaning for Peter and Gus.

Within a week of the workshop, this traffic light system was up and running and immediately the management team knew to channel their efforts into sales and away from production. This

CASE STUDY

focus on sales, especially to existing clients, will keep Eco Plastics in business.

The sales team can access the Beast remotely and are able to negotiate pricing with the solid knowledge of what products they can sell profitably. The Beast also allows them to experiment with *What if?* scenarios, allowing Gus to flesh out his idea for a waste by-product.

Within two months of the workshop Eco Plastics had stabilised and started to improve the balance sheet. The management team was now working together to source scrap and sell more products. As a result of their increased confidence in their decision making impact, they are further expanding their information sources to start identifying the biggest cost opportunity. Peter, Gus and Kate have harnessed their Beast and are back in control of their business.

A message from the authors

May the Beast be with you.

The authors

First and foremost, we hope you enjoyed reading *Harness the Beast!* We are passionate about our topic and want to help the world wake up to the huge potential surrounding us all.

We recognise that some people will say we are over simplifying a complex subject, that every Beast is different and you can't approach them in the same way. We strongly challenge this opinion.

People everywhere are discouraged from tackling this issue when faced with ever-changing technical jargon to explain the simplest of operations. We have purposefully used the simple metaphor of the Beast to open up the issue, to remove the fear and enable anyone to get involved.

The full utilisation of technology no longer rests with the technically minded but with the manager struggling to understand the monthly cost report, with the data clerk frustrated at repeatedly correcting the same error, and with the CEO wondering where to find the return for the huge technology spend.

It is time to stop the tail wagging the dog (or perhaps more appropriately, the Beast wagging the business) and for all of us to take on the responsibility of making the most of our assets.

Our plea is for you to challenge the status quo. Talk with friends and colleagues about the potential you see. Look for the divide and proactively bridge it. But don't expect everything to change overnight. You will need to have ongoing conversations with other like-minded people to change ingrained mindsets.

We have purposely written the book for the individual, as it is individual thinking that is critical in putting the Beast to work. However, where individuals will realise extraordinary wins, a company-wide change in thinking will create true competitive advantage. After all, every business has the opportunity to purchase the same technology; it is what the business makes of it that counts.

Your feedback on the book is welcome and we invite you to email us through the Beast's website: www.harnessthebeast.com.

Good luck and may the Beast be with you!

Chris and Anton

Appendices

Digital Health Check

> *Visionary companies do everything possible to make the company stronger tomorrow than it is today.*
>
> Collins & Porras
> Built to Last

The Digital Health Check provides a quick and easy indication of the latent potential available in your organisation and the size of business/Beastkeeper divide which you must overcome.

There are two sets of fifteen questions. The first set relates to issues around the latent potential and the second relates to the business/Beastkeeper divide. Of course, without having worked through the application of the rules, you may not necessarily be aware of all your Beastkeepers, so just answer the questions to the best of your knowledge. Following each question set is a score sheet to record your answers and tally your scores.

Once you have the two scores, use them to plot your position on the graph provided and then read what this plot point indicates about your organisation.

The questionnaire that follows here will take about fifteen minutes to complete. Alternatively, you could complete it electronically, and have our Beast tally your results, by visiting www.harnessthebeast.com.

Questionnaire

Circle ONE answer only in each of the following questions.

1. **Do you feel your company has helped you to make the most of the technology that it now has available?**

   a. Yes

   b. No

   c. Don't know

2. **Select the answer that best describes your personal technology inventory.**

   a. PC, connected to network, connected to internet, with access to major business systems that I need

   b. PC, connected to network, connected to internet

   c. PC, connected to network

   d. PC

   e. Nothing

3. **Does your company have telephone conferencing and videoconferencing facilities that you have access to?**

   a. Both

   b. Telephone or videoconferencing facilities

   c. Neither

4. **Do you have access to Beastkeepers who could help you?**

   a. Yes, I can access a huge team of Beastkeepers

   b. Yes, I can access a reasonable number of Beastkeepers

   c. Yes, I have limited access to Beastkeepers

   d. Yes, there are Beastkeepers but also reasons preventing me from using them

   e. No, I have no access to Beastkeepers

5. **Do you store information locally, accessible only to yourself, that might be beneficial to others?**

   a. Yes, I have lots of information

   b. Yes, I have a reasonable amount of information

   c. Yes, I have a little information

   d. No, I don't have any such information

6. **Can you think of information that, if provided earlier, would help you make much better business decisions?**

   a. Yes, I can think of lots of information

   b. Yes, I can think of a reasonable amount of information

   c. Yes, I can think of some information

   d, No, I can't think of any such information

7. **Is there information that you or your colleagues don't have that could significantly benefit your work?**

   a. I can think of lots of information

   b. I can think of some information

   c. I can think of a little information

   d. I can't think of any information

8. **Do you think there are opportunities for reducing the amount of travel you do by using videoconferencing rather that in-person meetings?**

   a. Yes, many opportunities each month

   b. Yes, some opportunities each month

   c. Yes, perhaps a few opportunities each quarter

   d. Yes, perhaps a few opportunities each year

   e. No, no opportunities

9. **Do you feel you spend time trying to answer questions that the company has answered many times before?**

   a. All the time

   b. Sometimes

   c. Rarely

   d. Not at all

10. **Do you feel opportunities exist for you, or the business, to respond faster with the right information, timely delivered?**

   a. Yes, many opportunities

   b. Yes, some opportunities

   c. Yes, one or two opportunities

   d. No, no opportunities

11. If you manage people, do you feel opportunities exist for empowering your team by giving them information that can help them achieve better results at their jobs?

a. Yes, many opportunities

b. Yes, some opportunities

c. Yes, one or two opportunities

d. No, no opportunities

e. I don't manage people

12. How much time do you spend chasing information from other departments within the company that could be reduced if it was available for you online?

a. A lot, more than four hours a week

b. A reasonable amount, between one and four hours a week

c. A little, one hour or less a week

d. None

13. Do you think there are opportunities to reduce the amount of information that is entered more than once into systems?

a. Yes, many opportunities

b. Yes, some opportunities

c. Yes, one or two opportunities

d. No, no opportunities

14. Having read this book can you see opportunities to reduce your workload with the help of Beastkeepers?

a. Yes, I can already see lots of significant opportunities

b. Yes, I can see quite a few significant opportunities

c. Yes, I can see some opportunities

d. No, I can't see any opportunities, but I'm sure they exist

e. No, I don't think there are any opportunities

15. Having read this book, can you see opportunities to improve the business with the help of Beastkeepers?

a. Yes, I can already see lots of significant opportunities

b. Yes, I can see quite a few significant opportunities

c. Yes, I can see some opportunities

d. No, I can't see any opportunities, but I'm sure they exist

e. No, I don't think there are any opportunities

Score sheet 1: The size of the opportunity

Mark your score in the **Your Score** box for each question.

Q	a	b	c	d	e	Your Score
			Your Answer			
1	1	5	3			
2	5	4	3	2	1	
3	5	4	1			
4	5	4	3	2	1	
5	5	4	3	1		
6	5	4	3	1		
7	5	4	3	1		
8	5	4	3	2	1	
9	5	4	2	1		
10	5	4	3	1		
11	5	4	3	1	3	
12	5	4	3	1		
13	5	4	3	1		
14	5	4	3	2	1	
15	5	4	3	2	1	
Total: Questions 1 to 15						

16. How great do you believe the divide is in your business?

a. Very great, an infinite chasm

b. Great

c. Medium sized

d. Small

e. There is no divide

17. Do the objectives of the Beastkeepers include making the best use of existing technology?

a. Yes

b. No

c. Not sure

18. How strongly do you agree that your organisation encourages you and your colleagues to work with the Beastkeepers to help improve the business?

a. Agree very strongly

b. Agree

c. Neither agree nor disagree

d. Disagree

e. Disagree very strongly

19. Do you know the names of the key Beastkeepers in your area?

a. Yes, all of them

b. Yes, some of them

c. No

20. How would you describe your working relationship with your Beastkeepers?

a. Excellent, we enjoy working together

b. Good, we work together well

c. Okay, we are capable of working together

d. Not very good, we don't work well together

e. Non-existent, we try to avoid each other

21. How frequently do you speak to Beastkeepers about your business goals?

a. Very frequently, usually every week

b. Frequently, more than once a month

c. Now and again, once every few months

d. Rarely, perhaps once every six months

e. Never

22. How frequently do you approach Beastkeepers to help you with non-Beast problems?

a. Very frequently, usually every week

b. Frequently, more than once a month

c. Now and again, once every few months

d. Rarely, perhaps once ever six months

e. Never

23. How frequently do Beastkeepers approach you to discuss how they can help you?

a. Very frequently, usually every week

b. Frequently, more than once a month

c. Now and again, once every few months

d. Rarely, perhaps once ever six months

e. Never

24. How confident are you that Beastkeepers know your business issues and goals?

a. Very confident

b. Mildly confident

c. Not sure

d. Not confident at all

e. Certain they wouldn't know

25. Where are most of the Beastkeepers that you might want to work with located?

a. Close by, on your site

b. On your site but a distance away

c. At another site, close by

d. At another site, a long way away

e. I don't know

26. Does your company employ your Beastkeepers?

a. Virtually all of them work for my company

b. Most of them work for my company

c. Some of them work for my company

d. Most of them work for another company

e. All of them work for another company

27. If your Beastkeepers work for another company, does this prevent you from working with them?

a. No, it's as if they work for us

b. Sometimes

c. Yes, it is very difficult to work with them

d. I don't know

e. They don't work for another company

How strongly do you think your colleagues would agree with the following statements (28 – 30)?

28. The role of Beastkeepers who work with us is primarily to fix and maintain our systems.

a. Agree very strongly

b. Agree strongly

c. Neither agree nor disagree

d. Disagree

e. Disagree strongly.

29. Beastkeepers wouldn't have the time to help us with our business problems.

a. Agree very strongly

b. Agree strongly

c. Neither agree nor disagree

d. Disagree

e. Disagree strongly

30. The Beastkeepers we see wouldn't have the skills to help solve my business problems.

a. Agree very strongly

b. Agree strongly

c. Neither agree nor disagree

d. Disagree

e. Disagree strongly

Score sheet 2: The size of the divide

Mark your score in the **Your Score** box for each question.

Q	a	b	c	d	e	Your Score
			Your Answer			
16	5	4	3	2	1	
17	5	1	3			
18	1	2	3	4	5	
19	1	3	5			
20	1	2	3	4	5	
21	1	2	3	4	5	
22	1	2	3	4	5	
23	1	2	3	4	5	
24	1	2	3	4	5	
25	1	2	3	5	3	
26	1	2	3	4	5	
27	1	3	5	2	2	
28	5	4	3	2	1	
29	5	4	3	2	1	
30	5	4	3	2	1	
Total: Questions 16 to 30						

Plotting your scores

You now have two results. The total from Score Sheet 1 reflects the latent potential available to you and the total from Score Sheet 2 reflects the size of the business/Beastkeeper divide.

On the graph opposite, the horizontal axis depicts the latent potential – the higher your Score Sheet 1 total, the greater the potential opportunities for you and your organisation to benefit from bridging the divide.

The vertical axis depicts the size of the divide - the higher your Score Sheet 2 total, the greater the business/Beastkeeper divide in your organisation.

Now use your two scores to plot your position. Then, read on to learn what this position indicates about your organisation.

Your Organisation

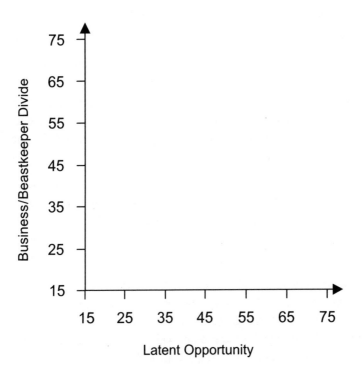

Poor Prospects

If your plot position is within or around the area highlighted in the graph opposite, it could mean one of three things:

1 you miscalculated the potential benefits of bridging the divide, or

2 your Beast is very small, without a Beastkeeper to call its own, or

3 you have already made the gains.

There's no way of knowing if you have miscalculated the potential benefits. If you have a very wide divide then it's possible that you are so much a part of the divide that you cannot see the opportunities. If this could be you, then take the initiative and approach your Beastkeepers. Ask them to consider how they can help you solve a crucial business problem, or achieve an important business goal.

If you work for a small establishment and your business technology infrastructure and resources are small or non-existent, then perhaps your opportunities are limited. If so, as long as you remain small, this may not matter. Remember though, if you have to start competing against organisations with an effective Beast, you could be in trouble.

Alternatively, if you have already made the gains, it is unlikely that attempts to bridge the divide will have a major impact on your business. However, this probably indicates that your divide is narrow anyway so your organisation is doing well. If you are working in one of these companies, well done. Yours is probably a harnessed Beast.

Poor Prospects

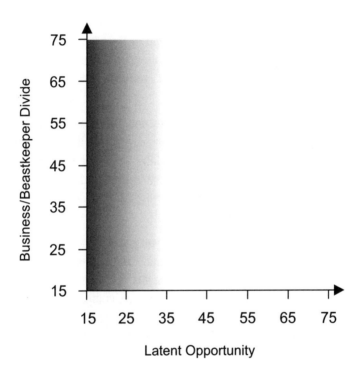

Good Potential

If your plot position is in or around the area highlighted in the graph opposite then good potential exists, however it may require some effort to realise it.

This position indicates that your company has a significant divide that will require considerable organisational effort to bridge. Personal attempts to jump the gap are likely to end in frustration. Having said this, depending how far to the right on the graph your company was positioned, there could be a lot of sensible reasons to start constructing that bridge.

It is highly likely that in this company the Beastkeepers and the business are alienated, and rarely work together. This means that trying to get the two groups to start working together could take a lot of time and effort. To gain full benefit, the organisation is certainly going to have to take responsibility for trying to bridge the divide. This won't be a job for you alone.

If you think the benefits are worthwhile, you can still attempt to reduce your own divide. If you can get some wins on the board, the organisation might start to see the benefits of trying to bridge the divide. If not, this may not be such a progressive company to work for. Remember, the companies that will win over the long haul will be those that derive maximum value from their resources, of which the Beast is a substantial component.

Good Potential

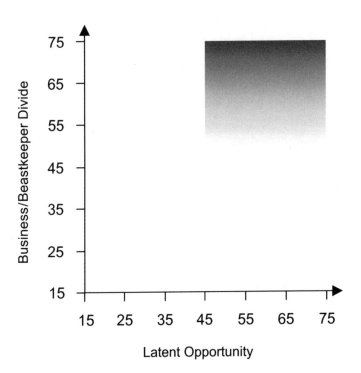

Rapid Improvement

If your plot position is in or around the area highlighted in the graph opposite then you should expect to achieve rapid and significant improvement.

Companies in this category are sitting on a potential goldmine if the organisation can bridge the divide and enable their people to harness the Beast. It reflects an organisation with two traits.

Firstly, the organisation will have a divide. However, it will be possible to bridge it. This is good news because it means even as an individual you can get started straight away. It also means that it shouldn't take long to make real progress. You can certainly set about bridging your personal divide immediately.

The second trait this category reflects is that it is likely the organisation has hidden opportunity. Depending on where you plotted your point, as your company bridges the divide, it will realise massive business benefits.

Given these two traits, a company in these circumstances, with a little effort, will yield savings quickly. As the divide is further reduced the company can significantly enhance its competitive position.

Go harness your Beast!

Rapid Improvement

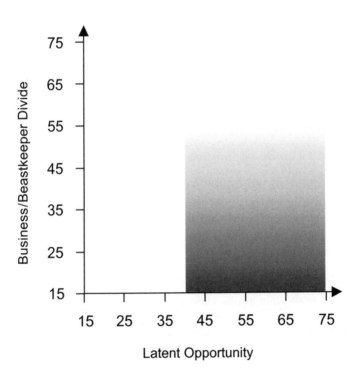

Index of case studies

Rule One The Beast is Accessible

More wine please   Page 24
John created shelf plans for wine shops. By accessing warehouse information on sales, he improved the shelf plans and increased wine sales.

Making it happen   Page 28
Daniel and Charles ran a boutique management consultancy. By accessing information from both their accounts and marketing systems, they better understood the levers on their business and were able to alter their priorities to improve profitability.

Rule Two The Beast is Alive

'Going digital' is not digital thinking   Page 41
Jane, the data processing clerk, thought she'd optimised her performance. However, by asking for live information, rather than waiting for a post-mortem report, Jane and her team increased their performance by 23 percent within a week.

But smelters are different... aren't they?   Page 44
Steve was responsible for the safety of seven hundred people, yet crucial safety information wasn't reaching the shift supervisors quickly enough. He solved his problem by making the safety information available live on the company's intranet.

Rule Three The Beast is Mobile

When 'going mobile' isn't thinking mobile   Page 53
Sebastian sold agricultural insurance on one continent but his underwriters were located on another continent. By reframing the situation to imagine the underwriters in an office next door, Sebastian and his people were able to improve their quotation speed and secure more business.

Packing sweets the boundary-busting way   Page 59
Mike had to reduce the cost of a case of sweets his company manufactured. Success came when he accessed knowledge from his counterparts in other company owned factories around the world.

Rule Four The Beast is Responsive

Quick, answer that call!   Page 68

Kim's call centre responded well to users' calls. Derek's team responded well to users' feedback on training courses. However, while each was optimising their response, the organisation's needs were being sub-optimised.

A supply-chain mesh   Page 77

Bill and George imported televisions and video recorders and distributed them to a major supermarket chain. Unfortunately, a disconnect between the importing and repair functions within their business caused major delays up and down their supply-chain.

Rule Five The Beast is Empowering

Milking the cash cow   Page 86

Angela's shareholders were pushing her to find a way of increasing the profits of a yeast distribution company. By establishing the size of the prize, her sales manager knew to change his sales team's bonus system from revenue to profit and to empower his staff to make the best deals.

Crisp action   Page 93

Jeff had to solve his waste water pump problem before his group general manager's visit. Was it the poor design of the waste water system, a faulty pump, a training problem or a bad patch of potatoes? The Beast empowered Jeff to make the right decision and solve his problem.

Soggy biscuits   Page 99

Rejected biscuits were par for the course until someone valued the loss at £140,000 a year. That was enough to empower maintenance to find the cause of the problem ... and a solution!

Windows of opportunity   Page 100

A large multi-national company was attempting to migrate 120,000 PCs worldwide. The Beastkeepers, trying to heed company policy, were contemplating running parallel servers and would have done so, until someone valued the cost of doing this at US$30million.

Rule Six The Beast Communicates

Talk takes time   Page 107

The organisation's push towards peer networking was overwhelming William with communication tasks. The Beast enabled him to communicate more effectively and in a way that saved him time.

Speed up by speaking up Page 113

Casey needed to make more bags every day, with the same equipment and number of people, to reduce the unit cost of production. Billy used his Beast to capture the best set up details for each machine. That way they could be shared effectively with all the operators.

Rule Seven The Beast is Efficient

Fresh outlook Page 125

Mel had to book project meetings for fifteen teams of editors, over 150 people, for the whole of the following year. She was determined to change the process or change jobs. In the end, she enlisted her Beastkeeper and together they dramatically improved the process and subsequently won an internal award for business excellence.

Asian crisis Page 130

Jeanne, the Human Resources manager was struggling to balance the training costs from the HR system and finance system. Eventually she consulted her Beastkeepers who got her and her Beast working more efficiently.

Glossary

The Beast

The Beast is a metaphor for the business technology in your company: computers, telecommunications, call centres, databases, applications, systems, networks, intranets, or any other piece of technology peculiar to your business.

- The **unharnessed Beast** is fat and lazy. It gobbles all your data and resources but gives little in return. An unharnessed Beast is a burden you carry.

- The **harnessed Beast** is sleek and fast. It saves you time and money, reduces hassle and errors, and generally improves your performance. The harnessed Beast carries your business ahead of the competition.

Beastkeepers

Broadly speaking, Beastkeepers are the people who care for the various components of your Beast.

- Typically, a **technical Beastkeeper** would be found in an information technology department performing any number of different tasks relating to Beast care and maintenance.

- **Information Beastkeepers** are more slippery to pin down but generally they manage the Beast's output. Therefore an information Beastkeeper might be the finance director, or an office clerk - pretty much anyone who really knows how to access the Beast but not how to maintain it.

The Business/Beastkeeper Divide

This divide refers to the lack of understanding and communication that occurs between business people and Beastkeepers, in a *never the twain shall meet* kind of way.

The Rules

There are seven rules for changing your assumptions about what is possible in order to harness your Beast. Opportunities for improvement can be found by identifying rule violations.

Digital Thinkers

People who believe in the rules, and consistently apply them, are known as digital thinkers. The act of automatically approaching any task, process, problem or goal with the rules in mind, is known as digital thinking.

Digital Health Check

The digital health check is a questionnaire for assessing the size of the opportunity within your business and the size of your business/Beastkeeper divide. It can be completed online at www.harnessthebeast.com.

Acknowledgements

We'd like to thank Martin for the Beast metaphor and Geoff for linking us up to David who brought the Beast to life. Thanks to Clive for connecting us to Middlesex University Press and Eileen for insisting we trouble the Troubleshooter.

Thanks also to Peter, Gus and Kate (you know who you are even though we fictionalised you) and our mate Pete for absolutely everything. Finally, a big thank you to all those who generously read the draft and provided feedback that subsequently improved the end product.